YOUTH MINISTRY
IN THIS SEASON OF
DISRUPTION

MARK OESTREICHER, GENERAL EDITOR
WITH CONTRIBUTIONS FROM
SEAN MCDOWELL, ANDREW ROOT, CRYSTAL CHIANG, AND MORE

Youth Ministry in This Season of Disruption

Copyright © 2020 by The Youth Cartel

Publisher: Mark Oestreicher
Managing Editor: Sarah Hauge
Cover Design and Layout: Marilee Pankratz
Creative Director: Tony Fowchy

ISBN-13: 978-1-942145-57-8

The Youth Cartel, LLC
www.theyouthcartel.com
Email: info@theyouthcartel.com
Born in San Diego
Printed worldwide

CONTENTS

INTRODUCTION

PIVOT OR DIE

By Mark Oestreicher

In the first few months of 2020 I was just getting used to the fact that I'd recently survived prostate cancer. Then March and April reminded me what it was like to catch a medicine ball (remember those?) in junior high gym class: They knocked the wind out of me. I cancelled a trip to speak to European youth workers, in Greece, on less than a week's notice. Then I cancelled multiple trips for the youth worker coaching cohorts I lead around the country.

Then my mom got rushed to the hospital and was quickly diagnosed with COVID-19. A few days later, it was obvious when I was on the phone with my dad that he couldn't catch his breath; hours later he was also in a COVID-19 hospital unit. And a week later, both my parents died, two days apart.

During these weeks, I was attempting to continue engaging things that would be life-giving. One of those should have been my weekly involvement leading an eighth grade guys small group for the junior high ministry at my church. But, full disclosure, I think it was about the most demoralizing and life-sucking season of youth ministry in my forty years of doing this.

5

Going into this time, I'd co-led a wonderfully tiny small group—just four guys. The *other* eighth grade guys small group in our ministry happened to have all the guys who behaved like you would expect eighth grade guys to behave, and was more than twice the size of my group. But somehow God had graced me with four somewhat bookish guys (one of them was *super* bookish: he would carry around a huge leather lawyer's satchel full of college-level veterinary books, which he was reading; he was writing a book of philosophy; oh, and he wore a full Alexander Hamilton outfit—wig included—every week in the first semester, and a three-piece suit every week in the winter). After more than a year and a half of investment, we'd finally gotten to the point where they were consistent, honest, curious, and mutually supportive. They asked great questions. And they prayed for each other. I was walking on clouds each week, after we met, in January and February.

And then I wasn't.

Only one of the four guys ever engaged with our Zoom groups. My co-leader and I started a group text with our group, and after each guy confirmed that, yes, his number was correct, he never responded again. Not once. Attendance was so bad in the youth ministry overall that our four total junior high guys groups met as one single Zoom group, and attendance at that dramatically dwindled week to week. With only one of my guys attending, I felt completely useless.

Our ministry leaders—we happened to be in an interim time between junior high pastors, but had an awesome intern providing energy, coordination, and direction—weren't the problem. There was just. No. Wind. In. My. Sails.

As I write this, in early September, I'm about to get a new seventh grade guys small group in five days. We'll be meeting, as so many of you are, in the church parking lot. I'm hopeful. But I know we will likely only see a fraction of the guys we would have in "normal times."

I don't do youth ministry well during pandemics.

THE THREE STAGES OF YOUTH MINISTRY IN THE PANDEMIC, SO FAR

- Stage one (roughly late March through late April, 2020): **Action**
- Stage two (roughly late April through the summer, 2020): **Discouragement**
- Stage three (fall 2020): **Innovation**

Remember how successful youth workers felt about two weeks after quarantine began? There was a mad dash to move everything online. Across the country, youth workers are often (though not always) the most tech-savvy people on any given church staff. So not only were you figuring out Zoom and livestreaming and all sorts of other technologies for *replicating* your programs online, many of you were tapped to help the church figure out solutions (Senior Pastor: "I'll do the preaching, you do 'other tasks as assigned'").

I led a handful of online youth ministry seminars a few weeks into the quarantine, and it was already passé to instruct people to try Zoom (or other platforms). After a few weeks of scrambling like mad, I observed a momentary period of "We've got this!" My day job is mostly about leading coaching cohorts with youth workers, and while people were certainly looking for ideas—mostly fun ideas (the pandemic version of "I need a new game")—the majority of youth ministries were doing something that felt like it was working. For a few weeks.

If I'd polled 100 youth workers, though, by the end of April 2020, ninety-nine of them were finding all the speedbumps you likely did: decreasing numbers, Zoom fatigue, regular attenders disappearing into the ether, and the wider community of "new" kids completely unreachable. "We've got this" turned to "This isn't working" faster than the attention-span limit of a sixth grade boy.

Panic turned to scramble turned to momentary confidence, which shortly gave way to discouragement. In the constant conversations

7

I have with youth workers all over the country, most of this past summer has been marked by discouragement and a strong sense of unknowing. I noticed a gap arise between youth workers' calling to connect in meaningful ways with teenagers and what they were actually able to do.

As difficult as this second stage has been, I am so incredibly encouraged by our tribe. Here's why: We concluded we can't return, this fall, to the approaches that proved less-than-satisfying in the spring—and this is giving birth to more innovation, in a short span of time, than I've seen in all my years of youth ministry.

MY PROJECTIONS

Things are changing so quickly, I'm going to invite you into a little futuring experiment. Back in late April, I wrote a list of Youth Ministry Projections based on what I was observing at the time. It's interesting to look back on—only a bit more than *four months later*—and see where I was wrong and where I might have been right. Here's that list from *way back then*, along with a bit of current-day commentary:

- *Our current use of Zoom and other online activities will not result in a massive re-imagination of youth ministry once we're completely past quarantine. We'll have some new tools in our belt, and that's good. But there's too much frustration with current approaches to call this a hinge-point.*

  Four months later: First, I think it's precious that I clearly assumed we'd be out of the pandemic by now. Aw, innocent little Marko. But, yes—this one holds true: Zoom is proving to be a new tool in our kit (and will continue to be, even after the pandemic is actually over in…I don't know…roughly forever more days), but it's not the wonder drug many prognosticated it would be.

- *It IS possible, however, that significant innovation could arise out of this next stage—in the months when we're not back to whatever "normal" was before quarantine, and when we're experimenting with "only in smaller numbers" limitations.*

Four months later: Almost got this one. I'm now suggesting, as you've read, that a second stage of Discouragement followed the time when I wrote this. And then, yes, we are now entering a pretty freaking amazing season of experimentation and innovation.

- *Speaking of this next stage, as states start to slowly open up: Even if youth ministries have no limitations (which will only be true in some states by June 1), many parents will be understandably skittish about sending off their teens to any large gathering (and for some, any gathering at all). This will provide much more of a challenge than learning how to log into Zoom or how to "mute all." If your youth ministry is more than ten students, you'll be forced to innovate (which will be hard, but could lead to good stuff).*

Four months later: Ignoring the obvious details I had wrong, this is absolutely one of the biggest challenges many youth workers will face in the coming twelve months. We might come up with good, safe ways to meet in person, but will parents allow their teens to attend? Of course, some will. But many won't. And if the current virus predictions for the winter of 2020/21 come true, this will grow as a challenge, rather than ebb away.

- *Many are already learning that good, online, produced content is not connecting with a large percentage of teenagers. Thoughtful youth workers are currently building new systems to leverage old, tried-and-true approaches to connecting with teenagers: texts, calls, snail mail, even gift drops. I'm hopeful that some of these systems will outlast our current limitations.*

Four months later: Yes, yes! You'll see these themes (both that well-produced content isn't enough, and that good ol' intentional contact ministry is critical) surface multiple times in the chapters of this book.

- *Church-based ministry with remote college students, however, will have some new means of connecting with students year-round. In almost every coaching cohort I lead, someone asks about how to connect with the college students who are mostly away at non-local colleges and universities. Many of these youth workers have concluded that gathering at Christmas and over the summer are their only options. Now they know this limitation was merely a façade.*

   Four months later: I think this one holds true. We'll have to see. What "going to college" actually means at this moment only matches the chaos of Christmas morning in a large family (but way less fun).

- *Many churches (especially larger churches) are going to weather this storm just fine, financially. But many churches will feel the financial impact of these challenging days for 18-24 months. Some churches won't make it (though this is likely only an accelerator toward death for churches that are already in trouble, whether they acknowledge it or not). Budgets will be limited. Spending will be cautious. This could force some needed innovation, but it won't be fun.*

   Four months later: The part of this I got wrong isn't actually in my wording here. What has surprised me is how many churches are doing *very well*, financially, through this season. For the simple majority (like, over 50%) of churches I interact with, giving is either steady or up, while expenses and spending are way down. However, churches are being massively cautious—even fearful—about spending. In one sense, this is prudent. But I truly wish those churches would just loosen up a bit, trusting more (I mean, trusting God, of course, but also trusting based on giving patterns these last six months).

- *Paid roles in youth ministry will most certainly decrease. They already are, and I hear about youth workers losing their jobs left and right for budget reasons. This is not a new thing—giving*

*in churches has been declining for years, and was projected
to continue declining well into the future as people shift their
giving patterns in our culture (mostly due to the departure of
institutional loyalty and the reduction of the role of church in
society). So this "tightening" is an accelerator. We may see a
small amount of rebound on giving, post-quarantine, but—as
Mark DeVries has been saying for years—many youth workers
will have to find other funding or other means of living into their
calling.*

Four months later: Yup, lots of paid youth workers are losing
their jobs right now. The projection I'd change here, though,
is that I now don't expect to see a rebound in youth worker
hiring. Churches will be uber-cautious on spending long
enough that it will become their new normal.

- *Youth ministry-supporting orgs (camps, short-term missions
orgs, coaching, training) and freelancers (speakers, musicians)
are going to be decimated. Maybe some change was needed
here, but this is particularly sad to me. Without summer events,
camps and short-term missions orgs are holding on by a thread.
And without a bailout (I don't mean a government bailout—I
mean either a massive donation or cash reserves amounting
to an endowment), many will be forced to close. With a large
percentage of church budgets tight for a long time, those
freelancers who rely solely on churches won't survive and will
have to redirect, vocationally. Even your favorite Cartel is very
much at risk: As of this writing, we haven't received a PPP loan
yet, and I'm increasingly concerned about our ability to make it
to the fall (I haven't given up hope, though!).*

Four months later: We got our PPP loan! But we (The Youth
Cartel) are so, so far away from being out of the woods.
Government loans and cutbacks and high levels of courage
and creativity have kept some youth ministry-serving
organizations (camps, missions, training, etc.) alive so far,
though certainly some have sadly reached an end. But unless
churches free up spending (which I think unlikely), these next

twelve to eighteen months are going to be absolutely brutal for hundreds of ministries. And freelancers, like speakers and musicians? Ugh—just praying they all find another source of income, as this one's not coming back quickly.

WHY THIS BOOK, AND WHY NOW?

The youth workers I'm engaged with need help. And they need massive doses of encouragement. This book starts with the assumption that you also need both of those.

For a few months, I had the beginnings of an idea for some sort of resource to address these needs on a low simmer. And one Tuesday morning in early September (9/1/20, to be exact), the framework for this book came to me (Thanks, God!), and a sense of urgency that *now was the time*. I experienced about fifteen seconds of regret that we hadn't initiated this project months earlier. But that regret was quickly replaced by a sense that we didn't know enough until now.

Our little publishing team has taken this book from concept to printer in one month's time—unheard of in the publishing world (normally close to two years). This rapid cycle was necessary to get a book out that's timely and helpful. However, it also means you, the reader, are asked to give us a teaspoon of extra grace: You might notice one or two more errors than normal, and had we had more time, I would have found a greater diversity of writers (though I'm pleased with the diversity we did find), and been a bit more intentional about things like a uniformity of chapter structures.

While doing my general edits, I chose *not* to edit the wording writers employed for teenagers—so you'll see a mishmash of youth, teens, teenagers, young people, and students. I tried to keep both the *voice* and contextual language of the contributors intact. My hope is that this will actually be a strength of the book, rather than a stumbling block for readers. We assume you are smart enough to contextualize what you read for your own needs.

I also chose not to include any chapters on ideas that pretty much all youth workers have figured out by now. So you won't, for example, see a chapter on how to screen-share in Zoom. I don't expect you'll connect with every single chapter, either. But I hope you'll find a couple of chapters that deeply encourage you—and I hope you'll find a couple of chapters that spark your imagination to try new things.

Let's do this!

Do not give in to despair! Youth ministry is hard right now; it *has been* hard for longer than we thought it would be, and it *will be* hard for longer than we'd assumed. But youth ministry is needed as much as ever (more, in many ways). We're just gonna have to get creative. And remember: Hope starts with lament. Then, with honesty and open hands, we follow the whisper of the Spirit's leading. God is with you, and with every teenager you love (and even the ones who drive you crazy).

Marko, September 2020

Mark Oestreicher has been working with teenagers for forty years. Marko is the founder of The Youth Cartel, providing resources and coaching for youth workers.

SECTION ONE

A HISTORICAL ENCOURAGEMENT

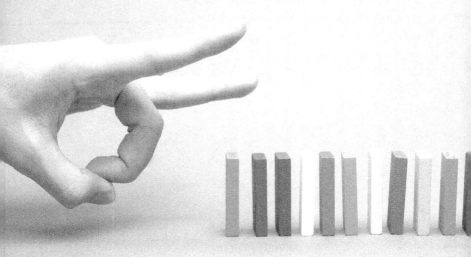

DISRUPTION IS NOTHING NEW

By Dr. Sean McDowell

My world was turned upside down on March 13, 2020. And I know *yours* was too.

It was 6:30 a.m., and I was unloading my bags at the Orange County airport, heading to speak at a Disciple Now (DNOW) weekend in South Carolina. My wife called, and I answered the phone expecting her to wish me well on my trip. But there was an *urgency* in her voice that took me by surprise.

"Have you been listening to the news?" she asked. "This outbreak looks serious, and I think you might want to reconsider taking this trip." I sat there for a few moments, prayerfully trying to decide if I should go or not. The youth pastor had been planning this for months, alongside a number of other churches, and I didn't want to be the one who messed it up!

After listening to the news, and weighing the caution of my wife, I decided it was probably best not to go on the trip. I called the youth pastor in charge, and even though they had planned the entire event around my messages, he was gracious and understanding. But I still felt like I was *that guy*.

It turns out they cancelled the event anyway. And for me, it wasn't just that event—my entire speaking ministry was disrupted. Some events went virtual, which I am thankful for, but a huge part of my ministry, which helps support my family, unraveled overnight.

Please don't hear me complaining. I'm not. I realize that a ton of people, and probably many of you reading this, have had your lives and ministries disrupted by COVID-19 far more deeply than I have. My point is that, in a sense, *we are all in this together*. We have all had our ministry plans and strategies disrupted and are now asking some difficult and challenging questions:

- When will things get back to normal?
- Will there be a new normal?
- How can I reach and disciple kids in this new era?
- How can I minister in a post-COVID-19 world?

I can't pretend to have answers to these questions. But I can share three principles that have helped me pivot my ministry during a season of disruption.

PRINCIPLE #1: THE CHURCH IS NOT GOING ANYWHERE

First, I have clung to these words of Jesus: "I will build my church, and the gates of hell shall not prevail against it" (Matthew 16:18, ESV). Essentially, Jesus is saying that he will build a community that will prevail against all opposition.[1] If the gates of hell cannot overturn the church, then neither shall persecution, heresy, or a global pandemic!

Something else stands out powerfully from this passage: Jesus is the one who will build the church, and it is *his* church. He is the one who owns the church *and* the one who makes it grow. Is it possible that God is using this pandemic to shear the American church of its false pretenses and focus? As painful as it can be for all of us, I have to trust (and hope) that God may be disciplining his church to become more strategically effective and also more reflective of his character.

PRINCIPLE #2: WE ARE IN GOOD COMPANY

The second principle that has helped me pivot my ministry efforts is the reality that the church has been adapting to disruption since its inception. Simply put, *our experience today is nothing new*! Sure, there are some unique elements of our times, but the church has experienced a long line of culture-changing shifts that it has successfully adapted to. Let's consider three examples:

Disruption #1: The Debate Over Circumcision. The biggest disruption the early church faced was the question of the continual application of the Law for believing Jews and Gentile converts. For over 1,400 years—which is *a lot* of generations—the Jewish people had been relating to God through observance of the Old Testament laws. Sabbath. Sacrifices. Passover. Circumcision. The rhythm of their lives, and their identity as a people group, were tied to their observance of the Law. And then all of a sudden, non-Jews could join the community of God without observing the Law? Can you see how disruptive this might be?

This clash is what led up to the Jerusalem Council (AD 48). Specifically, some people were teaching that circumcision was required for salvation. To make a long story short, the apostles affirmed that salvation is by grace, but for the sake of unity, they agreed on a compromise: Gentile converts would not need to be circumcised, but should "abstain from the things polluted by idols, and from sexual immorality, and from what has been strangled, and from blood" (Acts 15:20b, ESV).

This council was pivotal for the early church, but such debates continued for *decades*. When seen through modern eyes, it is easy to miss how radical a disruption this was for the first Christians. From the perspective of believing Jews, it was earth-shattering. Yet the church adapted through time, patience, biblical teaching, and the creative compromise offered by James.

Disruption #2: Persecution from Rome. Another radical disruption for the church was when persecution broke out in Rome. The first Christians were often protected from Rome as long as Christianity was considered a sect within Judaism. But in the time of Nero (AD 54-68), Christianity became an illegal and suspect religion whose followers experienced disgust, mistreatment, and sometimes death at the hands of the Roman Empire.[2]

Perhaps the most prominent reason was that Christians refused to pay homage to the Roman gods. Because the gods were considered the guardians of Rome, protection for the Roman people required they be given their proper honor and respect. In refusing to worship the Roman gods, Christians were considered unpatriotic and dangerous. According to church father Tertullian, when tragedy hit, the collective cry was for Christians to be thrown to the lions.[3]

How did the early Christians respond? Their primary response was to *respect pagan authorities, pay their taxes, and be good citizens.* In his epistle written to those who were suffering, Peter writes, "Honor everyone. Love the brotherhood. Fear God. Honor the emperor" (1 Peter 2:17, ESV). Christians also responded by offering an apologetic to the Roman Empire about why the charges against them were false.[4]

Disruption #3: The Church Gains Power (Constantine). The church went through another radical disruption in the fourth century with the rise of Constantine. He enacted laws in favor of Christianity and had churches built. While it's a myth that he made Christianity the official religion of Rome, he did favor Christianity and ended persecution.

How would the church respond to its newfound favoritism? Sadly, the response was mixed. Some Christians committed violence against pagans. Some leaders became arrogant and corrupt. Many Christians combined pagan and Christian beliefs. And yet because martyrdom was no longer possible, many devout followers headed to the desert, as part of the monastic movement, to "sacrifice" their lives for the faith.[5]

These are only three examples of the many disruptions the church has experienced since its inception. Just think about all the other disruptions, such as the collapse of Rome, the Renaissance, the invention of the printing press, Darwinism, the Sexual Revolution,

the rise of communism, integration in the 1950s and 60s, World Wars, and so on. Virtually *every* generation since the time of Christ has faced the same question we face today, namely, "How do we do ministry in a time of disruption?" We are in good company.

PRINCIPLE #3: KEEP MINISTERING

The third principle that has helped me pivot my ministry efforts is to focus on the importance of ministry *during* a season of disruption. As a teenager, C.S. Lewis served as an infantryman in the trenches of World War I. When World War II hit, he offered some reflections for Christians that are timely for today.

> Yet war [the coronavirus] does do something to death. It forces us to remember it. The only reason why the cancer at sixty or the paralysis at seventy-five do not bother us is that we forget them. War [the pandemic] makes death real to us, and that would have been regarded as one of its blessings by most of the great Christians of the past. They thought it good for us to be always aware of our mortality. I am inclined to think they were right.

> All the animal life in us, all schemes of happiness that centered in this world, were always doomed to a final frustration. In ordinary times only a wise man can realize it. Now the stupidest of us know. We see unmistakably the sort of universe in which we have all along been living and must come to terms with it. If we had foolish un-Christian hopes about human culture, they are now shattered. If we thought we were building up a heaven on earth, if we looked for something that would turn the present world from a place of pilgrimage into a permanent city satisfying the soul of man, we are disillusioned, and not a moment too soon. But if we thought that for some souls, and at some times, the life of learning, humbly offered to God, was, in its own small way, one of the appointed approaches to the Divine reality and the Divine beauty which we hope to enjoy hereafter, we can think so still.[6]

When my ministry was disrupted by Coronavirus, I remember

thinking, "Okay, I can't speak to students on stage anymore. How will I reach them? How can I pivot and still minister to young people?" For me, that meant starting a TikTok account, building my YouTube channel (which is more focused on youth influencers and apologists), and writing another book for students.

I don't know what that means for you. I am not a youth pastor, so I won't pretend to give you advice. But I know this: God promises his church will prevail. We are in good company. And ministry matters deeply during this season.

Let's do this *together*.

Sean McDowell, Ph.D., is a professor of Apologetics at Biola University. He is the author of over twenty books and uses Twitter, Instagram, and a bunch of other social media platforms.

A THEOLOGICAL ENCOURAGEMENT

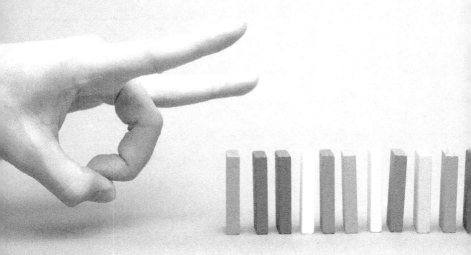

HERE AND NOW

By Dr. Andrew Root

When my latest book was published just prior to the pandemic, my publisher and I thought that its title—*The End of Youth Ministry?*—would be provocative enough to draw attention. We never thought that it would be prophetic.

Now, several months into the pandemic, for most congregations and para-church organizations, youth ministry has, indeed, ended—at least, it has ended in all the ways that we have always done youth ministry (not being allowed to gather in groups larger than ten will do that).

My book asks a question, which is not often wrestled with by youth workers, pastors, and youth ministry gurus: Why do youth ministry at all? It asks what youth ministry is really for. These questions were important before COVID-19 had locked us in our houses, maxing out our bandwidth. Now, these questions are existential.

The question "What is youth ministry for?" is important, particularly in middle-class settings, because, during the past decade or so, congregational youth ministry has not fared very well. The waning of youth ministry has not, however, been caused by a frontal attack: There have not been petitions or speeches calling for the ending of youth ministry.

Rather, next to all other opportunities and activities in teenagers' lives, youth ministry has slid down the scale of importance; just ask any youth worker. In the autumn, parents make a commitment to getting their children to a youth group or confirmation class, but when things get busy in October, the same parents tell youth workers that their child just does not have time. Basketball, test preparation, piano practice, or any other dozen activities will keep them from participating in youth group activities. During the past two decades, the youth group has lost its prominent place in families' schedules.

Ironically and counterintuitively, however, this slide seems to be concurrent with parental involvement. Over the past generation or so, as parents have become more involved in their children's activities, youth ministry has had less hold over families' time and attention. We could say that young people are less committed to youth groups not because parents are less concerned for the future of their children, but because they are more concerned.

Over these past few decades, we have seen a whole reworking of our imagination of a good life. Once—indeed, as recently as the 1980s and '90s—parents believed that they gave their children a good life by staying away: Providing ample free time and free space gave an adolescent what they needed to flourish, it was believed.

This is evident in the Netflix drama *Stranger Things*, which readers would do well to watch during their quarantine. In it, Mr. and Mrs. Wheeler, the parents of Mike, one of the main characters, are classic (and loving) 1980s parents, who stay out of their teenagers' lives. In the era depicted, a parent's job is to provide meals, a basement, and a curfew. Outside of that, children are free to roam the neighborhood. If you happen to be in Hawkins, the small Indiana town where the series is set, your roaming will include fighting a demogorgon. If not, you may find it advantageous to go to a church youth group, have some mindless fun, and hang out with some friends. There wasn't much else to do in the 1980s.

There has been a radical shift since then. Today, a good parent is considered to be one who helps his or her child to flourish, who no longer stays out of the child's life, but organizes and directs it. Parents now see it as their responsibility to help their adolescent children flourish by giving them every opportunity to find themselves by finding their thing (cheerleading, singing, dance, chess) in the world. Schedules are no longer open, but packed with practices and tutors (so packed that they drive parents to exhaustion).

But that is all worth it, it is believed, because that it is how you become a good parent. Today, a parent's job is to help their children live whatever dream they want in the future—by getting them involved in all the right activities, practices, and rehearsals. It is frantic involvement that will do it.

The German social theorist Hartmut Rosa argues that people's lives have been so sped up over the past few decades, going faster and faster, that they no longer have any sense of what a good life is in the present.

We have no sense that it is our job to help our kids understand and live the content of a good life now. Even Christian parents are not sure what the good life is. They are even less sure how they would teach and form their child toward a good life that's for the here and now. The present, Rosa explains, is too short: Our lives move too fast for us to assume that a good life has any content in the present.

The good—what it means to flourish—has shifted almost completely into the future. Parents drive thousands of miles from one sports tournament to the next, or across the county or state for lessons with the best piano teacher, not because they believe time in a smelly minivan is part of the good life. They do it because these activities give their child resources. And, if they get it right, those resources can be cashed in for a good life in some undefined future.

Youth ministry will never be able to compete as an activity. It will never rival sports or music, because it can never promise to give young people the kind of resources that can achieve some future dream. While saying things about the future, Christianity particularly is—as all religious traditions are—more concerned about the present. There is a sense of ultimacy about the future, a hope for the beyond; but faith is about what it means to live in this moment. Faithfulness is living fully in relation to God now.

So, what in the world should youth ministry be for in this time of contagion and quarantine? Imagine that your whole life as an adolescent, or as a parent of an adolescent, has been about "looking forward": to the next competition, admission to an elite university, being chosen for this team and playing in that tournament, how you'll juggle both your children's tournaments on the same day.

Now, just imagine that one day (as we all experienced months ago), all the "looking forward" was suddenly over: All the work, investment, time, scheduling, and momentum halted. Imagine that all the activities that produced resources toward giving your child some future good life stopped. And imagine that there was no timetable for when you could again "look forward." Your whole identity as a parent, and an adolescent, was found in "looking forward." But now there is no way to do so. Who are you?

What do you do when a virus causes you to be completely and relentlessly in the moment? How do you live only with enough knowledge (and schedule) for the present? What is the purpose of life, of parenting, if all your control in setting what's coming and what needs to be looked forward to, is over? You can't even crawl back to the youth group, the ever-reliable backup activity, waiting in the wings.

When the trappings of youth ministry end, what we are left with is the core: ministry. Right now, this is where youth ministry has to start: in the painful gift of being given the here and now. What we can offer parents and young people is an invitation to be in the present and to reflect on what it means to be living well.

It is in this unique moment that youth ministry can ask young people to respond. Perhaps churches could invite them to make videos and micro podcasts that wrestle with what it feels like to be in the here and now. What makes it full or meaningful? What is it like to stop and listen for the voice of God, not in "looking forward," but right now, in the pain now? This moment gives us an odd (and poignant) opportunity to ask young people who they are, where God reaches for them.

At this time, youth ministry needs to be exposing young people to stories of people in their church communities who have found God in moments of longing and loss, of hope and hardship. What about pairing them up with an older member of the congregation to interview? "Tell me about a hard or strange time: How did you sense God in it? How did it change you?"

It is in these very moments, when "looking forward" has no power to pacify and distract us from our being alive, that we need to seek for the God of life. Youth ministry now needs to wonder: What if all the things that we were looking forward to never come again? How will we grieve for them? But, more importantly, who will we be? Who is God calling us to be now? Asking these questions together— that's what youth ministry is for.

First published in Church Times, 17th April 2020.

Dr. Andrew Root is Professor of Youth and Family Ministry at Luther Seminary, St Paul, Minnesota, in the United States. His latest book is The End of Youth Ministry? Why parents don't really care about youth groups and what youth workers should do about it.

SECTION THREE

ISSUES TO THINK ABOUT

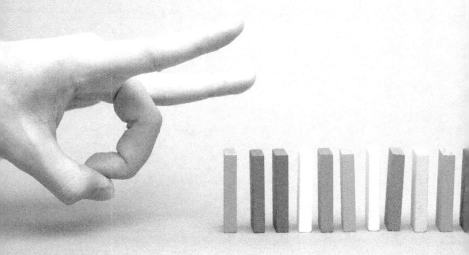

LONELINESS & HUMAN CONNECTION

By Crystal Chiang

As a middle schooler, I had a single dream: to live in a town with a shopping mall.

Clearly, I've always dreamed big.

Before you judge me, let me explain. In the 1990s, smack in the middle of my adolescent years, malls were the epicenter of teenage life—or at least I thought they were. While living in a rural community made mall visits rare, I watched television shows and read magazines about teenagers making after-school mall trips and I was pretty sure that I was missing out big time.

Maybe you grew up in an urban or suburban area where after-school mall trips were part of your daily experience. You understand how the noise, the conversation, the sale at Claire's and the smell of fresh-baked mall pretzels mixed with the cologne cloud coming out of an Abercrombie & Fitch store can produce euphoria. If you wanted to find teenagers, you went to the mall. They were always there…

Until they weren't.

There is no shortage of articles about malls dying in America. Fewer are being built. Some are closing. Some are transforming into sports complexes or distribution facilities, and while there are plenty of theories about *why* this is happening, the reality remains that the institution I once imagined to be the anchor of teenage social life no longer is—at least not in the same way. **The rules of how and where and *why* teenagers gather have changed**, leading marketers and retailers back to the drawing board to reimagine what happens in the next decade.

In some ways, youth ministry during the disruption of this pandemic feels a little like we're all sitting at that same drawing board. That's not to say the practice of youth ministry is an antiquated or dying mall (youth ministry may be more important than ever), but the rules have definitely changed. What worked before doesn't always work in this new reality. What made sense before in our games, in our worship, and in our sermons doesn't necessarily have the same effect on a Zoom call or seated in the church parking lot six feet apart. Something has changed. In addition to plenty of other responsibilities, **youth workers in the age of disruption must reimagine how and when and where and *why* teenagers gather.**

Despite how Twitter makes it seem, there are no "experts" in how to handle this new reality. None of us has been here long enough to claim to know the best way forward. At best, we are explorers, learning from one another as we journey into new territory. For the past few months, I've been talking with youth workers around the US (and in a few other countries) as we reimagine life in this new reality. I've noticed the same question keeps coming up:

What do we do about human connection? More practically, how do we think about, and plan for, socially-distanced versions of…

- games
- worship sets
- sermons
- streaming strategies
- in-person and online environments

How do we make sure we continue to create more than an online program? In other words, how do we create opportunities for the powerful human connections that used to happen in person? *And is that even possible in digital and socially-distant spaces?*

It's a fair question. After all, a large part of the transformational quality of youth ministry has always been connected to the relational and human connections it provides. Most of us know from our own faith experience that…

Connection has always mattered.

For many of us, our own faith journeys were shaped by a connection with another person or group of people.

In addition to our own experience, over and over, research reminds us that community is essential to faith formation, and a teenager's faith is most likely to grow in an environment where they are connected to one (or more) caring adults and a consistent community of peers.[7]

I think this question of human connection comes up so often in conversation because many of us have a sneaking suspicion that, while it has always mattered, **connection matters now more than ever.**

In this entirely new global reality, none of us knows for sure how teenagers will be affected, but what we do know for sure is that loneliness was a public health crisis long before COVID-19.[8] Add to that a rise in teenage anxiety and depression, difficult home circumstances, academic pressure, the general human trauma that comes with surviving this year, and the needs for a student to feel

seen
heard
loved
believed
known

are all more important than they've ever been. In fact, **maybe more than anything else we work toward in our ministries, we must prioritize finding ways for students to connect with each other and with leaders**—even if that means rethinking all the ways this used to look. Even if it means...

- Changing the program
- Moving to a small group strategy
- Finding more volunteer leaders
- Meeting in backyards
- Meeting with masks on
- Meeting in digital spaces where every student can be seen and heard

To be honest, I don't know whether shopping malls are going to be around in ten years or if teenagers will want to hang out there, but I suspect, if they do, it won't be because the mall-creators have changed the décor, added trendier stores, paid for blinking LED signage, or updated the food court. **It will be because other teenagers are there (and the possibility of connection is high).**

In that way, we have a lot in common.

What kept students engaged in most of our ministries for the last few decades wasn't our environments, our signage, our most-relevant sermons, or even snacks after the service. Those were important, but they were never the main event. It was always about the possibility of connection.

The most effective youth ministries have always prioritized what happens in relationship over what happens on stage. So, as we explore together and discover new ways to do youth ministry in the age of disruption, we would be wise to prioritize what is most powerful in our ministries and put "opportunities for connection" at the very top of our to-do lists.

Crystal Chiang is the Executive Director of Student Strategy at Orange. She lives in Atlanta with her husband, Tom, and an embarrassingly ill-tempered chihuahua named Javier.

CHURCH POLITICS AND WORLDVIEW TENSIONS
By Andrew Esqueda

Clearly you are aware that our country is currently rife with political divisiveness. We are hit with politics from every angle: in the news we confront, the social media we devour, among family members, in athletics, in education, in medicine, and no less significantly among these, in church. There's something that feels hopeful yet ultimately naive in thinking that the church would be beyond political division—the political atmosphere of our country escapes no one. Throw an uprising of what some are calling a new civil rights movement[9] into the middle of a global pandemic and we've got a blender full of political, religious, and social ideologies, and no one seems to want to take a drink. But, to avoid this blender would be to reject the reality that the people we minister to and alongside live in contexts bombarded (and often determined) by these realities and worldviews.

Not least among those affected by this cultural divide are young people. Youth workers of all stripes have seen the impact this disruptive state has had on the psyches of young people, and many have attempted to address the disruption in ways that put the spiritual and emotional health of youth at the forefront. But even this attempt is a huge feat for youth workers as the church is undoubtedly one of the messiest political places to exist. The pandemic has caused the majority of churches to physically close;

some have decided to reopen, some are still closed, and others are somewhere in between. Similarly, some churches have spoken out against racial injustice, some churches have spoken out against the protests, and many churches aren't sure what to say. This has put youth workers in a precarious position, one that has employment, programmatic, and relational implications. So, in light of varying worldviews and political opinions, a global pandemic, and the ever-looming specter of church politics, what is a youth worker to do?

First, give yourself permission to simply do *something*. There's constant pressure that we youth workers often feel—that we have to get it right all the time, because we believe the stakes are so high. You don't have to solve the political disruptions we encounter, change anyone's worldview, or perfectly navigate the waters of church politics. And you don't have to get it right every time. But, to *not* address polarizing subjects with the youth you minister to is to ignore the real world in which they live. Do something! A program, a conversation series, a relevant topic for youth group—and do it in a way that embodies Jesus's words in Matthew 6 instructing us to be salt and light. Your burden is not to change the minds and worldviews of your youth or ministry context, it's to **be faithful to the gospel and to engage in meaningful and challenging conversations**.

Second, church politics are real, and you may be on a different page than your congregation or head pastor. That's okay. Find people who will support you and who will join in the conversation about seeking to be salt and light to your youth. I work in a mainline denomination where the orderly following of policies and procedures is paramount to getting anything done. Whether you work in a similar context or a different one, your governing structure can be your friend here. In June, I was preaching at our live-streamed service and I felt compelled to pointedly ask, "Is it not the job of the church to ensure that black lives and brown lives matter?" There were certainly people in the congregation upset I said this from the pulpit, but as a brown person myself, the question needed to be asked of a denomination that is 90% white.[10] I felt confident saying this knowing I would have the full support of my oversight committee. Notice, I didn't say the full *agreement*, I said the *support*—because my leadership committee knows that my primary motivation is not politics, but the gospel. Agreement shouldn't be our motivation for ministry, but faithfulness should, and what an example we set for our youth when we take the risk of living out our faithfulness to Christ.

Third, if you're going to take on the challenge of doing youth ministry in a politically divided church and world, then you must seek to answer the question, **What is youth ministry for?** In large part, I think Andy Root answers this question rightly in his fantastic book *The End of Youth Ministry?*: It's for "joy."[11] I want to tweak that a tiny bit, due to the divided nature of the social context we live in. Youth ministry is for joy, but not merely "I as an individual have joy in Christ." Rather, what I want to live into, and have my teenagers experience, is "I'm finding joy as I seek to promote joy in the lives of others."

When we think about finding joy in Christ, it shouldn't be joy in isolation from other people.[12]

And when youth ministry is understood to be for "joy seeking out joy in and for others," the divisive and disruptive nature of the political climate and church politics ceases to have ultimate power over the important ministry youth workers engage in daily. Joy is challenging because it requires us to find ourselves in Christ. Those who have found their joy in Christ can no longer look at global pandemics, police brutality, racial injustices, and their differently-opinionated friend or relative through the eyes of politics. Instead, they have to view them through the eyes of Christ, considering what it means to love God and neighbor, for any other posture is antithetical to what the Christian means when they speak of joy.

Establishing a youth ministry grounded in joy makes the first two steps easier and more fulfilling, but it's also the hardest part because it is an attack upon our own desire to establish our ministries ourselves, rather than cede them to Christ. However, this task is worth it because in the face of disruptive politics in culture and church, the joy found in Christ becomes the ultimate disrupter, requiring an unqualified love of God and neighbor.

Andrew Esqueda is the Associate Pastor of Family Ministry at Trinity Presbyterian Church and the host of the podcast, The FormationCast. He lives in Atlanta, GA, with his wife, Megan, sons, Isaiah and Desmond, and an English Bulldog named Cali.

INTEGRATION AND COMMUNITY

By Sam Halverson

I heard about a church with a financial "nest egg" its members had accumulated through the years. It was a designated account stashed away in a bank somewhere—its purpose being for a day down the road when troubles arose and the church needed the funds, a "rainy day" fund, a treasure, waiting to be used.

Well, eventually it rained.

It actually poured. A heavy recession happened; church membership declined; bills needed to be paid; giving was down. A storm had developed.

The crazy thing was, the congregation decided those rainy days were not the ones for which the fund was intended. Some believed the treasure should stay in the bank—they should hold out for a stronger storm that was sure to come eventually. Others forgot there was such a fund, it had been locked away for so long.

So the fund sat there during those rainy, stormy days. The investment became worthless because no one used it.

How great is a treasure if no one uses it?

The youth in our congregations are the treasure of our churches, and when we refuse to use our young people, we miss out on enjoying the investment. The storm comes. The time passes. What is substantial becomes worthless. The treasure is lost or, in the case of our youth, might quickly cease to believe it is valuable to the congregation.

During this season of disruption, I have seen congregations "hunker down," ignoring the treasure they have in their youth by keeping them separate from other ministries. Integrating youth into the entire church body is essential if we are to realize the investment of the treasure God has given us, and we have an excellent opportunity to start something new. We currently have plenty of reasons to ask people to try different things, but instead we have quarantined youth into separate Zoom rooms and virtual studies where they no longer experience what it means to be one part of the body of Christ, working in unity with other members.

Integrating youth into the whole life of the congregation is how congregations thrive. Jesus said if we are to experience the kingdom of God we must become like children (Mark 10:13-16). How can people expect to approach their faith like children unless they get to know the young among them? Helping our congregations integrate with teenagers fosters insight and understanding for everyone involved. Youth learn from watching and seeing (and hearing the stories of) adults; conversely, adults realize the expectation, mystery, trust, and sometimes doubt it takes to lead to stronger faith. We learn from each other and the insights of others.

Advocating for the integration of youth in the body of Christ is a hard position to hold in easy times, so it's understandable that in a storm we might falter out of fear. Being locked away in a pandemic makes it difficult to build this integration—at least, in the ways we are used to. When everyone meets in person, we have chance encounters between youth and adults. Once the storm comes, though, even "in person" gatherings stay within the confines of their age groups or the small, secure groupings we need to maintain safety (if they meet at all).

If we approach the hard times with fear, we will ignore the richness of the treasure we have in our youth and miss the opportunities youth can offer in bringing us through the storm. But if we approach each disaster or threat as an opportunity for something new, allowing for failure and learning, we will ask new questions, come up with new answers and new ideas, and move into areas of ministry we had only dreamed of going with our youth.

Start encouraging your church leadership to tap into the investment of its youth. Ask lots of questions about what ministry needs are met (and which ones aren't) in your neighborhood and look for ways youth can partner with older members in meeting them.

Your task as a youth worker is to help the congregation minister with the youth (not to do it yourself). The best way to do that is to get youth involved with members of the church outside youth ministry programming. (After all, we want our youth to step into other church ministries when they are no longer teenagers.)

What if every youth had a relationship with a multiple adults in the church? Imagine being confident that every youth was prayed for daily—by name—by the adults in your congregation. What would it take for your youth to be confident in knowing such prayer is happening? What would a celebration of a year of intentional prayer for every youth look like?

Look for ways to involve your youth in the planning and carrying out of ministries during this strange time. Some of your ministries involve knowledge originally not needed (tech for online worship, for example); are there some youth who show interest and leadership in such opportunities? Do you have youth visibly present in every online worship experience? What if a few youth and a few adults were to host the chat before or after each online service, giving them a goal of engaging each observer and being available for some Q&A?

The key to plugging youth into these ministry opportunities is not finding new jobs for younger people—it's the relationships you are building between the adults and the youth. Your online worship might not *need* any more volunteers, but if youth are not present in such a ministry they won't feel a part of it. You may have enough adults serving with the small gatherings, but unless you seek out ways to introduce other congregation members into telling their stories or offering their skills, your youth might never come to appreciate the vast knowledge and experience of the body of Christ.

Use the strangeness of this pandemic to invite youth into these new relationships. Encourage adults to involve youth in planning and offering new ideas. Unearth the treasure. It's raining, and now is a good time to show others what youth can do.

Sam Halverson is an ordained United Methodist elder currently serving as Associate Director of the Office for Congregational Excellence for the North Georgia Conference, directing and resourcing youth ministries for the conference. Sam is author of three books for youth ministry; the most recent is One Body: Integrating Teenagers Into the Life of Your Church.

SAFETY

By Jeremy Steele

In the second week in youth ministry via Zoom, a youth worker sent me a text asking, "How does our child safety and abuse prevention policy apply to Zoom?" I sat back in my chair and looked up at the ceiling, realizing that I had never seen a policy in my denomination that covered the new world of exclusively digital ministry that we were living in every day.

That's task number one for this chapter: How do we protect students from predatory behavior in our online ministries? Task number two will be to explore how we move through the migration from online to in-person (and maybe back again) in the age of the pandemic.

Safe Sanctuary in Digital Ministry. Underlying basically every child abuse and prevention policy is the idea that everything done in your youth room (as opposed to a public space like Starbucks) with teens needs to have two unrelated, non-cohabitating adults involved. When a large group is broken down into smaller groups in a large facility, there needs to be easy access to the areas where the small groups are meeting. Most policies also allow for a "floater" in this situation. It allows you to have one adult per small group room with another adult "floating" around in the facility monitoring what is going on in the rooms.

The two-adult rule is all about minimizing the risk of harm to the youth in your group. It ensures that teens will never be placed in a situation where they are having to make a report of inappropriate behavior where there is not another adult to back up their account. It should never be an adult's word against a youth's word as to what happened. When the two-adult rule is followed, there is a second, adult witness to the behavior that is being reported. Now that we have that groundwork laid, let's walk through how this applies to our digital ministry.

Two Adults and Zoom. That two-adult rule has to apply to your online meeting space as well. If you are having an online meeting via Zoom, Google Meet, or—if your IT person really doesn't like you—Webex, you must have a second, non-cohabitating adult in the meeting with you. For that to happen, they need to be logged into the meeting before the students so that students don't enter a room with an adult by themselves. This rule should apply to any online space where you are in a live, synchronous situation with teens including Facebook live chat or other similar experiences.

If you employ breakout rooms, there should be two non-related, non-cohabitating adults in each of them. If there aren't enough adults to make that happen, you need to have a person with host privileges who is actively "floating" from room to room to check in on what's happening.

Two Adults on Accounts. The two-adult rule should also extend to your official social media accounts. Those accounts should have multiple people with administrator rights or multiple people with the password to the account depending on how the platform handles administration. Simply having access is not enough. People with access should be expected to log in and look at what has been going on periodically and without prior warning.

Making Social Media Connections. In person when an adult is exhibiting predatory behavior, or just being generally creepy, it's easy for other adults to see, and can be easy for a student to simply walk away. That is not the case online, which requires us to set some boundaries for how social media connections are made.

There's an unequal power dynamic between a youth and a youth worker. That can translate into youth feeling obligated to connect or engage with those adults online. To avoid putting youth in situations where they feel like they have to engage with an adult against their desire, social media connections (friending, following, etc.) should always be initiated by the youth.

Though this is not necessarily something you can or should try to police, setting the expectation with youth, parents, and volunteers will help people see when someone is pushing the boundaries, and will give everyone a way to describe the digital lines that have been crossed.

Private Messaging (DMing, Texting, Etc.). Private messaging, in general, should be discouraged in favor of more real-world interaction that follows the safe sanctuaries guidelines. When that is not practical or feasible, private messages should be kept to informational conversations like, "Don't forget about youth group this Sunday." When a text begins to be more conversational, the adult involved should quickly move it to a group chat, with the consent of the student, where another unrelated adult can see the conversation.

No matter what, private messaging should never happen on a platform where messages disappear by default (like Snapchat). Similarly, adults involved in the youth ministry should be instructed to never delete private messages with youth.

In-Person Safety in the Age of a Pandemic. As you move into and out of in-person gatherings in the age of a pandemic, your health protocol should be as carefully thought out as your lesson. Your state, and often your denomination, will have guidelines for how, when, and where you gather. Your policies should be well within the guidelines set forth by those bodies.

Before you gather, the people who are in charge of making sure the policy is followed should have that policy and know ahead of time they are responsible for making sure it's followed. Every community is different, but these are the areas every policy should consider:

1. *Symptom check.* Before students are granted access to the meeting, a symptom check should be performed by measurement (thermometer) and/or interview ("have you had a fever or cough before you arrived?"). Those symptoms should follow guidance of local and national health experts.

2. *Personal protective products.* Before the gathering, all participants and volunteers should be informed of what personal protective products they are required to have. You should make sure there are some disposable versions available on site for those who leave theirs at home.

3. *Clearly-defined, distanced spaces.* It's not enough to tell teens to stay six feet apart. Those distances must be clearly defined (tape on the ground, hula hoops in the grass, etc.) and enforced by the adult in charge of the policy (and ideally, by all adults).

4. *Bouncing noncompliant students.* Normally we do everything we can to keep students from being sent home, but when it comes to a pandemic, strict compliance needs to be expected and enforced. That will mean sending home students who refuse to follow the rules.

Safety is key whether you are in person or online, and when expectations are communicated clearly, these sorts of rules are comforting to youth, parents, and volunteers.

Jeremy Steele is the associate pastor at Los Altos UMC in Los Altos, CA, as well as a writer and speaker. You can find a list of his books, articles, and resources for churches, including his most recent book, All the Best Questions, *at his website: JeremyWords.com.*

FEAR & TEENAGE CATASTROPHIC THINKING
By Bethany Peerbolte

Three weeks into the COVID-19 pandemic I received a phone call from a youth in my church. They were in tears convinced they were going to hell. This idea was planted in their head by TikTok. With more time to scroll through this social app, the student had stumbled across Christians using apocalyptic texts in the Bible to condemn "lukewarm" Christians. I was baffled. In a time when we all felt anxious and helpless, these account owners decided the best use of the Bible was to infuse the world with more anxiety.

Of course, many teenagers are also struggling with fears about the impact of the pandemic on their own lives, or on those of their family and friends. In a lot of ways teens are uniquely equipped to relate to apocalyptic Scriptures. The vibe of Revelation is familiar to teens. Their daily recaps often sounds oddly like the biblical warnings. The head space from which we get dramatic summaries of prom is the same mindset John was in as he went to sleep that fateful night before his revelation. They are both results of catastrophic thinking. While catastrophic thinking can lead to extraordinary entrepreneurial success (I'm thinking of inspired creations like seatbelts, Life Alert, or Ring door cams), it can also lead to devastating pits of despair.

Catastrophic thinking is a hallmark of teenage life. A breakup easily becomes interpreted as the last time one will feel loved. A failed exam means a future dream job is gone before graduation. Worst-case scenarios often haunt the teenage mind, but catastrophizing can also be an immensely helpful behavior. It helps us stay aware of potential trouble so we can anticipate danger and make early adjustments to avoid the threat. Unfortunately, our brains are terrible at statistics. We can perceive 1,000 threats and 999 of them never come to pass. The one that does become a reality convinces us that the catastrophizing was worth the effort. This perpetuates the behavior of constantly scanning for threats, even though 999 of the perceived threats were wastes of energy. Catastrophizing feeds anxiety and shuts us off from new experiences and deeper relationships.

The Book of Revelation is the result of John's catastrophic thinking. John goes to bed concerned about the fate of the world. His mind is exhausted from trying to find the safest path forward, one that will not cause him harm. John assumes the worst and sees beasts and horsemen and plague. God gently helps unravel the chaos in John's mind by offering clarity and encouraging curiosity.[13]

Clarity. Catastrophic thinking thrives on hyper-focus. Catastrophic thinkers try to protect themselves from negative outcomes, so it pays to stay focused on the negative possibilities. Revelation, on its surface, feels like a negative text. It seems to be condemning and downright scary. We can see John's hyper-focus on terrible beasts and his desperation to see things from all possible angles.

God regulates John's hyper-focus with divine clarity. John finds such relief in the clarity of his dream that he must write it down. When he is catastrophizing again, and that time is near (Revelation 1:3), he wants to remember the insight God gave him. For us, the most important point of clarity comes in the first verse: This is a revelation. The Greek word John uses here is *apokalypsi*, and it means a type of literature that recounts a symbolic dream or vision that reveals God's perspective on history and current events, and how that perspective will affect the future. This point of clarification is important because it indicates that we are heading into a text that is full of symbols and double meanings. Apocalyptic writing begins with the assumption that readers will do the work of interpreting. John writes about beasts, but he means for us to hear about evil. He writes about the end of days, but he means for us to hear about the future that our history and current events will lead us toward.

When we encounter catastrophic thinking today, we can use God's method of clarity to help tease out the deeper meaning under the symbols catastrophic thinkers create. The symbol we encounter might not be monsters; it might be a person characterized as the bully. And in reality, this person might just be a bully, or there might be something bigger underneath. Our ally in interpreting all of this with teens is asking open-ended questions that can't be answered with "yes" or "no" or other one-word answers. Open-ended questions force us to think about an answer and formulate the sentence(s) that express ourselves. Ask about something the thinker has left out, or simply say, "tell me more." Any dialogue will help bring clarity to a mind that needs a rest.

Curiosity. The other fallacy in catastrophic thinking is assuming that we know the truth. In a state of catastrophic thinking, a person will fight against any information to the contrary. Catastrophic thinking is particularly good when it comes to self-defense. The whole point of catastrophic thinking is to protect the thinker from negative outcomes. Taking time to look at the bigger picture feels like opening the thinker up to attack. We can feel Revelation doing these kinds of hyper-focused dives. John goes on tangents giving many details about minor things all to avoid the bigger truth—the truth that there is grace.

Revelation models that one should engage all the facts. There are 184 direct quotes from Scripture in the revelation, some apocalyptic and some full of grace. John's revelation is literally urging us to reread the Bible. It's saying one needs to see the whole picture of Scripture to understand the symbols in the revelation. We can't just take what we read in the final book and yell about the end of days. We need to spend time in, and talk about, the whole Bible to understand Revelation's message.

As we encounter catastrophic thinking, we should encourage curiosity. Curiosity keeps a steady flow of new information to the mind and negates a stagnant, catastrophizing brain. We can model this for others who are stuck. We can create a space of positivity and love to allow them to openly wonder with us. Ask them about their friends, teachers, or pets. Ask "I wonder how [enter someone else's name here] feels or thinks right now." This helps to pull catastrophic thinkers out of their own experience and allows them to be curious about the experiences of others. This will reveal that there are other ways to process the experience. Hopefully they will encounter someone who has found a positive side to the same distressing time.

The most important lesson about catastrophizing we can take from Revelation is that challenges need to come with encouragement. It does take challenges to grow, but a challenge alone is never enough. Encouragement makes the challenge safe to work through. God's grace is what allows us to leave catastrophic thinking behind and face the world with clarity and curiosity.

Helping youth connect their stories with God's story has been Bethany Peerbolte's call since 2008. Her favorite parts of youth ministry are the 2 a.m. conversations on retreats, the bus ride dance parties, and the constant supply of Capri Suns.

SECTION FOUR

MISSTEPS AND LEARNING

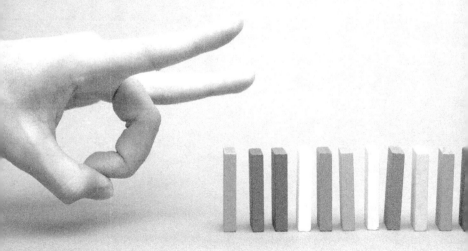

8

PARALYSIS OF ANALYSIS

By Danny Kwon

I did nothing for about six weeks. That was my ministry response when our church and youth ministry were suddenly shut down by the state of Pennsylvania in the middle of March. Perhaps it was because I was a skeptic and a doubter. Even after almost thirty years in ministry and twenty-seven years as the youth pastor at my present church, during which time I survived and persevered through many difficult things, I still wasn't really prepared for a pandemic of such proportions as COVID-19. Was anyone?

In retrospect, my six-week ministry work "paralysis" resulted from a lot more than just skepticism about how much a virus could impact our country and disrupt church ministry. It was certainly more than just a spiritual funk. Rather, it was like a deep morosity, combined with being lost, a feeling of fear, and perhaps even some evidence of a spiritual depression. I did not know what I should feel, nor was I able to identify what I was actually feeling, and I didn't realize the profound impact all of this had on me and our youth ministry.

One of my biggest fears—driving my sense of being lost—was represented by my wondering, "What am I going to do now?" Just before the shutdown, we were flourishing. We had a wonderful student leadership team, and four short-term mission team trips were set up, with months of meetings and training planned and scheduled. Our ministry volunteers were active and robust. My ministry parents were supportive. And I'd set up a calendar listing the spring events of our students. But suddenly, it was all gone. And what was left, I realize now, was the onset of a subtle but deep trauma for me: a sense of losing all of what had been built up over twenty-seven years of ministry at my church. So, I did nothing… then nothing…and then nothing. It wasn't a misstep in ministry due to the virus. It was a "no-step."

Looking back now at those weeks after our church closed, I realize what I was experiencing was ultimately a form of "paralysis of analysis." Probably more the "paralysis" part than the "analysis" part. Generally speaking, "paralysis of analysis" is a term that describes overthinking a situation to the point where decision-making can become paralyzed, and no course of action is decided upon or taken. Fear is often associated with a paralysis of analysis as, for example, one searches too long in hoping to make the perfect decision, or one worries about making a bad decision. In critical or crisis situations (like the sudden onset of a virus) when actions and decisions need to be reached more expediently, bigger issues can arise if decisions are not made, which, ironically, can lead to more paralysis, and consequently a lack of decision-making and action.

I write this as an authentic confession of a veteran youth worker. You don't survive twenty-seven years at one church without learning how to overcome many obstacles and disruptions. But still I sat around in paralysis and moped for those six weeks or so, not really knowing what to do. I share this knowing that while some youth workers have been wildly creative and successful with ministry ideas during this season, many feel like quitting or are burned out, feeling lost, isolated, and useless, and wondering when or if our ministries will recover. We are Zoomed-out with fatigue, working harder than ever, and some of us are getting deeply discouraged. Any of these things could be the source of your own paralysis, whether it's today or any other time. As we move ahead and continue attempting to figure out ministry during this pandemic, we are going to have good days and hard days, hopeful weeks and hopeless weeks.

Eventually, I wrestled out of my morose paralysis and found a bit of freedom by applying some lessons I'd learned over past years. I don't have all the answers, but I want to share with you the greatest and most helpful of those lessons: It is important to show yourself some grace—the grace that Jesus shows us—especially during this season. None of us has ever before done ministry during a pandemic. We are all experiencing the good and bad of it. We are all learning how to do ministry in a uniquely difficult season. So, embrace these difficult days of struggle and know we are all going through this unknown time together. It's not easy for anyone. But God is gracious to us, so show yourself some grace. Ultimately, it is this grace that will begin to set you free from the paralysis of this time and give you hope for continuing to persevere, try new things, and thrive.

Danny Kwon has been serving at Yuong Sang Church for twenty-seven years leading the Youth and Family Ministry, and teaches in the Youth Ministry Department at Eastern University. He completed his Ph.D. in Organizational Leadership and has authored three books.

9

RETHINKING SUCCESS

By Kevin Libick

By many metrics, we are a successful ministry. Or rather, before COVID-19 we *were* a successful ministry. We could draw a crowd. Our small groups were thriving. We had wonderful leaders. But all of this success was built on the ability to gather together.

Then the pandemic hit and took that ability away. Because we could no longer meet in large numbers, we couldn't do our worship gatherings. We couldn't continue our small group programs in the same way. We couldn't do large events.

So, like many youth ministries, we pivoted and went online. Zoom and YouTube became our new gathering spaces. Over time Zoom attendance and YouTube views plummeted, and this left our team defeated and frustrated. We scratched our heads wondering if we could do ministry in the new norm.

The reality is that we had a definition of success based on our numbers and it became clear to us that our definition was no longer viable.

When disruption happens, old models and definitions become invalid, not because they were bad to begin with, but because your world no longer looks the same. As a leader you can choose to RELY

on the old definitions of success by hoping the world will go back to "normal." You can become RESIGNED to the fact that the world has changed and you may never be able to achieve success again. Or, you can accept the new normal and REFORM your definition of success to fit the new reality. Which of these is most true of you?[14]

As a ministry, we had to strip away what we *thought* success was and redefine success based on our new reality.

In this season, one of the phrases I've been saying to my team over and over again is, "Don't focus on what you *can't* do, focus on what you *can* do." Doing the former makes us frustrated and paralyzed to make any progress. Doing the latter opens our minds to new paths of progress and changes our attitudes toward the disruption.

In ministry, our definitions of success are both comforting and daunting. Usually we define success based on what we know how to do well. Our church defined success by what we could count (attendance, number of leaders, registrations). These definitions are comforting because we know what to aim for.

However, our definitions of success are also daunting, because we base our worth on those definitions. Every youth worker knows the deflating experience of putting a ton of work into an event that bombs numerically. Riding the highs and lows of results-based success metrics is the reason why many youth workers walk away from ministry.

If you're experiencing this sort of frustration, maybe you need to redefine success for your ministry. Here's how to do that:

Define success based on your values. Your values are the things you believe to be essential to your ministry direction. They are reflected in your language, structure, and budget. What are your ministry values? Does your definition of success match those values? For us, we'd *say* we valued small groups as the core of our ministry, but there was a disconnect. We assumed more attendance was the same as small group success. If small groups really are the core of who we are, then we have to redefine success apart from gathering in physically-present groups.

Choose a definition of success based on input, not output. We like to define success based on numbers because we link our worth to those results. But this type of results-based success is not a reliable metric because we have little control over things like attendance. We can't control when a teacher assigns a test or a game gets rescheduled (all things that lead to a student not showing up).

We needed a new metric based on what we *can* control: an input-based definition of success. Input-based success metrics are things we can do that, over time, reflect our values of spiritual growth. Since small group community is a core value, we chose relational touch points as a new metric of success. In other words, success now meant doing things that led to people feeling connected.

We couldn't control when a student showed up, but we could control when *our leaders* showed up in the lives of students.

A new win for us became phone calls, one-on-one meetings, letters, and emails. Instead of getting students to show up, we wanted our staff and leaders to know that connecting to students and parents was our new win. We knew that if we reached out in these ways each week, our students would feel connected.

When disruption happens, you need to aim for something new. Redefining success based on your values and on inputs you can control is a pathway to thriving in the midst of chaos.

Kevin Libick is a longtime middle school youth worker and amateur BBQ pitmaster. He's passionate about helping other youth workers better live out their calling. Kevin lives in Texas (home to the best BBQ in the world) with his wife, Kara, and five-year-old ninja, Knox.

REMINDERS ABOUT SOUL-CARE AND IDENTITY
By Tandy Adams

Go to any city or small town in America in July and you'll see fireworks (most years, that is!). What makes fireworks fun is not only the fire (duh), but the display of power contained in such a small vessel. Once that fuse is lit, the firework is transformed when an explosion happens that propels it into the sky, where it creates beautiful displays. Americans spend upwards of three hundred million dollars a year on fireworks.

When COVID-19 hit, churches, and church leaders specifically, became fireworks. The fuse was lit and we were off: full steam ahead to create something beautiful and completely new. Suddenly we had to figure out how to create community and relationships while continuing to shepherd students and families in their faith journeys.

Because we have a holy calling to Jesus and his church, we took on this challenge full of enthusiasm and zeal. We created, we studied, we learned new technologies. We pivoted from all we knew, for the sake of the gospel.

The thing with a firework, though, is once the show is over, we are left with ruins. The clean-up takes longer than the set-up. The clean-up also requires more effort to pull off than the show. We started out as fireworks, but now we find ourselves in ruins. Not our churches, not our ministries, but our souls. This is why self-care matters.

John Wesley was known for opening meetings by asking a simple question: "How is it with your soul?" As church leaders we have often (and particularly in this season) neglected our souls. We have seen a need, we have pivoted, we have created beautiful things—but in all the busyness, in all the chaos, we have not taken the time to attend to our souls.

We have too often decided that if we work harder, if we are more productive, if we have more students or come up with new and even more creative ideas, then those external things will fill our internal needs. We lit the fuse and off we went. What's left now? The mess.

The core of who we are is our souls. And our ministries are dependent not on the best new idea, but on our souls.

It is time to clean up the mess.

Soul-care is not just about your relationship with Jesus or your walk with him. It is about your entire being. That truth begs the question: How do we practice soul-care? What follows are a just a few thoughts and ideas.

Be intentional with your Sabbath and your boundaries. It's not selfish to take an afternoon off, or even an entire day off. It's not selfish to turn off your phone for a few hours. It's not selfish to leave town for the weekend. These things are necessary. Spend time with Jesus, take a walk, go for a drive or to a baseball game. Put your Sabbath on the calendar and guard that time.

Surround yourself with people who make you happy. The best we can often do for our souls is to be discerning about who we spend time with and who gets our emotional energy. Spend your time with those who build you up, not those who drain you.

Remain focused on the big picture. God has called you and it is his work that sustains you. You were never expected to do ministry solely by your own power. What God started in you, he will complete.

Invest in professional help. Sometimes we need help to clean up the mess.

When I attend a firework show, I often leave thinking, "I could do that." I want to go and buy all the things and then try to pull it off at my house. But we all know that our abilities are often limited by our resources. Sometimes others can just do it better. In ministry, this is important to remember.

COVID-19 has youth workers sharing ideas and collaborating. It has also led to ministry envy at an obscene level. This envy has always existed. We often look at others who do something well and then try to recreate it. When it doesn't work, we're left feeling like we have failed. But your context, your gifts, and your calling are yours alone. The kingdom of God is vast and he has given each of us specific gifts. What works for me may not work for you. That truth speaks nothing of our abilities or our calling, regardless of how we may internalize it.

Part of practicing self-care is to focus on your identity. You are not the sum of what you do or don't do. You are not a title. You are not your job. Your worth has nothing to do with your performance. You are a beloved child of the God who created the universe, the God who loves you unconditionally and pours his grace out extravagantly. The God who walks every day in relationship with you. That's who you are. Perhaps the greatest act of soul-care is remembering this.

Tandy Adams is the Director of Family Ministries at Castleton UMC in Indianapolis. Her passions are baseball, the Cubs, and people...and guitars and Jesus.

REMEMBER TO LOVE THOSE WHO AREN'T SHOWING UP
By Ben Knox

Ministry leaders get mere minutes to shape how our teams will think about their role in students' lives. This is how I used my minutes for our church's team. What follows is adapted from a "vision talk" for adult leaders to launch a new ministry year. Like many, we made a quick pivot in March/April to online ministry, with mixed success. Heading into the summer, we checked in with students, parents, and leaders. We heard what worked and what flopped for different people, but more significantly, we heard how those people were doing. Based on what we've learned, we want to focus leaders' efforts on students' current needs. For those of us who coach other adult ministry leaders, everything below also applies to our relationships with those leaders. Love your whole list of leaders, even those who have to step back from their role for right now.

We have a temptation in this season to jump to questions like, "How do we do stuff on Zoom or from six feet apart?" Those are good questions, but they're not the first questions. First, we need to zoom out (pun intended; you're welcome) and ask a different question: What's our job here?

As leaders in student ministry, **the top line of our job description is to love students in Jesus's name.** That top line does *not* say, "facilitate a small-group discussion about the Bible." That's a big part

66

of our job description, but it's not the top line.

In a normal year, we could get away with some top-line confusion. We could trick ourselves into thinking that small-group discussion is the main thing—and in 2019, that might have turned out fine. In 2019, if I had thought "My job is to be a good small-group facilitator on Wednesday nights," that might have effectively communicated Jesus's love to students.

But 2020 isn't 2019. We can't get away with top-line confusion anymore. Life in a pandemic is not normal, and so we must keep our eyes on the top line of our job description, *or we will miss the target*. To do this well right now, we've got to **love our whole list of students, and not just when they show up.**

Your list might include students like these:

- You know her well from last year, but she's not showing up, because the pandemic has surfaced significant mental health challenges. She's too anxious to hop on another Zoom call, and what she really needs from you right now is to know that you care about her.

- He wants to come to small group...but he just forgets it's Wednesday! A gentle text reminder at 7:05 p.m. goes a long way.

- You don't know this student, because they've never shown up—they've never experienced Christ-centered community before. But this year, there's no basketball practice. A get-to-know-you chat with you on a random afternoon might give them the courage to show up on Wednesday.

- Her parents are recently divorced, and on Wednesdays, she's with the parent who thinks church is trash. That's why she's not showing up. You're connecting with her through an online journal.

- She's a student who's nervous about inviting her friend to church or to small group. Then one Tuesday, you exchange a couple direct messages with her when she's hanging out with that friend, who asks, "Who are you DMing?" One week later, there's one more person on your list.

- He's the oldest of four in a single-parent family, and mom's got cancer. Small group isn't always the place where he can be himself or feel seen.

If we suffer from confusion about what's on the top line of our job description, we could miss opportunities Jesus wants to give us to express his love to these students in 2020 and beyond. Our job is not primarily about Wednesday nights. Will we also do great stuff on Zoom or from six feet apart? Absolutely. Programming is going to be great, but it's not about programming. It's about loving students in Jesus's name.

So, as we start this fall, we will:

1. **Gather students' direct contact information.** Those with or without phones, all ages, with safe policies in place.

2. **Brainstorm connection ideas together**, thinking through options for leaders with different time margins.

3. **Try something.** If it flops or your time margins change, try something else.

Am I asking you to do something that will take some of your time outside regular ministry programming? Yes. I don't ask for this lightly. I'm asking because it's critical to the top line of our job description: to love students in Jesus's name. This year we've got to love our whole list of students, not just when they show up. If we do, we just might come out of the pandemic loving students better than we did on the way in.

Ben Knox is the Pastor of Middle School Ministry at Blackhawk Church in Madison, Wisconsin.

CELEBRATE THE AWESOME

By Jonathan Hobbs

I had friends move out to Colorado a few years ago. Soon after they settled in, they started exploring activities that their new home encouraged. Their Instagram overflowed with pictures of hiking excursions, lakes, mountains, and skiing trips. They were celebrating the awesomeness of their new reality.

Psychologists seem to agree that this sort of thing is a fantastic step for children who have moved. When someone is put into a new context, especially when the change was not of their choosing, it is important to celebrate the things that are now possible thanks to that new context. That is how people move forward.

I grew up in the Philadelphia area. After college, I moved to New Mexico. Instead of trying new things and exploring, I shut myself in and tried to recreate things that were familiar. I kept attempting to make cheesesteak sandwiches. They tasted horrible. Instead of celebrating the new I was settling for a bad version of the old.

I think that's what churches might be doing right now.

Instead of thinking through what possibilities we have in our new reality, we are using substitutes and pretending they're good enough. Instead of celebrating the awesome things about our new "home" and moving forward, we are inventing reasons to "get back to normal." I have even seen some interesting interpretations of Scripture being used to support this thinking.

I wonder if people who insist on returning to "what was" are feeling drained of creativity. Maybe an inner monologue is telling them they can never be anything more than what they were, nor can they ever learn a new skill. Maybe they are afraid that their talents and skills only applied in the context that no longer exists. No wonder they are tempted to manipulate things to go backward, or at least complain about how things used to be "better."

If we calm down and focus, we might start to see the new opportunities. Time constraints are pretty minimal in virtual contexts. We can take lunch to students who are doing virtual school. Speakers who would usually be too expensive to hire now might be able to record a message for an affordable price. There are lots of doors opening in front of us, and we're going to miss them if we just sit and grumble about the ones that are closing.

I personally failed hard in this area. We took our youth group online and I tried to do normal youth group things. It was horrendous. "New Mexican cheesesteaks" kind of terrible.

With my pride sufficiently wounded, I defaulted to grumbling. Half of my job was now firmly in the "other duties as assigned" column. When did I become a TV producer and camera operator? Why was I spending so much time editing videos? I also started lamenting not being able to do things that actually are in my job description. Mission trips and summer camps were gone and I was left feeling lost and useless. I began to believe my inner monologue and I wanted to get back to what felt safe and comfortable.

I have heard many of my friends in youth ministry express similar experiences. It hurts my heart so much because this should be our time to shine. Being creative and challenging the norm are things most youth workers live for! But I think many of us are experiencing at least some level of burnout. Not surprisingly, the creative juices are not flowing and the ideas are not coming.

It's not bad that you are doing a ton of things outside of your job description. It's all hands on deck right now and your church needs your voice and creativity in this time. But this can be incredibly exhausting. That's not because you are weak. It's because you jumped into the chaos like a boss. You need more rest. Get it. You need to let your mind relax. Spend time in stillness. If you hear voices creating a negative inner monologue, go full Daniel LaRusso and crane kick it in the face. You have not lost your skills. God called you into ministry knowing full well that this pandemic was coming.

This has the potential to be your most fruitful year of ministry, but to get there you need to stop trying to go backward. Christ has called you to ministry here and now. Your job description is going to be changing. We are off the grid now. It is time to blaze new trails. There are awesome new opportunities—and that's worth celebrating.

Jonathan Hobbs has worked in the field of youth ministry for over twenty years and currently serves at the Church of the Good Samaritan in Paoli, Pennsylvania. He and his wife, Carolyn, have two amazing daughters, and they all agree that his impression of Kermit the Frog is solidly mediocre.

13

BEING TRUE TO OUR CONTEXT
By Marty Estes

I sat in a pew in our old worship center with a group of deacons and other staff, listening to the tense-yet-friendly dialogue taking place. As many other churches considered closing their doors due to the pandemic, it was decision time. One day removed from Sunday, we all agreed that worship had felt "off" somehow, missing a key dynamic of warmth and fellowship that our congregation often enjoyed. I had been on stage that morning and watched as a family left because of someone coughing repeatedly behind them. Anxiety began to set in as we talked around the various issues within the issue. We already knew the decision we had to make; we just didn't want to say it.

I imagine my experience was like that of a lot of you who are reading this book right now. COVID-19 came on us quickly, and we responded by shutting our doors for ten weeks (or longer) and moving completely online. Having met earlier in the day with our staff, we knew that we would have to act fast to be ready for this new medium, and a fellow staff member and I began to dream up a way to produce online worship services, Bible studies, and more to meet the needs of our congregation. I was no longer simply a youth pastor, but had become a media pastor as well. And that's where the problem began.

What started as an idea to produce a weekly worship service, children's and youth videos, and adult Bible study soon became a source of frustration as our dreams for a slickly-produced video like other churches were able to create just didn't seem to win us viewership. Views started out strong and quickly dipped, which led us to ramp up our efforts in music, editing, and more. What I quickly came to understand is that in our rural community of seven thousand people, that simply wasn't what they wanted. We were failing in our mission because of a connection gap.

When people talk about our church, I have always heard them describe the feeling of warmth and connection that they have after attending. As a "big" church in a rural area, running two morning services until recently, creating this warmth and connection was a feat that seemed impossible. But somehow our people did it: They made others feel like part of the family from the moment they walked in. This was an "it factor" we tried to carry over into the DNA of our youth ministry, working to make sure first-time visitors were connected with an adult and another teenager as soon as they walked in. While our online services were as top notch as we could make them, and we tried to make our Wednesday night Bible studies just as engaging as if you were there in person, a key component was missing: authentic connection, the glue that held our church together from week to week.

I think we can all agree that it's incredibly difficult to be authentic from behind a computer screen, whether it's prerecorded or a video chat. There's a barrier there that doesn't exist when two people are in the same room, or a group is gathered. For me, I felt like I needed to perform, that I needed to have control, and most of all, that it needed to be excellently produced with over-the-top quality. Those kinds of performance-related tendencies are traps that blind us to the real need for authentic connection between us and the teenagers we minister to. When I realized that I was concentrating more on how the Zoom call looked, sounded, and went overall than on the people I was seeing on the screen, an alarm went off in my soul! I began to shift my thinking from production to connection. In my mind I saw frayed ends of rope, each strand connected to one of my students. How would we begin to tie these threads back together?

I wish I could tell you I had the bullet points all lined up for how we do that. As we creep toward meeting together again, I truly believe we will lose some of the students we ministered to before. You will, too. However, here's my prayer for all of us: Let's not forget that ministry is infinitely more about connection than production, lest we become like the Pharisees of old.

Marty Estes has been in full-time student ministry for the past eighteen years, and currently lives in rural West Tennessee with his wife, Erin, and children, Isaac and Annaliese. He loves bacon, Transformers, LEGO, Nintendo, and podcasting.

PAUSING FOR SURVIVAL

By Pat Villa

From the fear that trusting You will leave me more destitute, deliver me, Jesus. ("Litany of Trust"[15])

I'm afraid for you to read this chapter. I'm afraid you'll disagree with the choice I made. And that you'll think less of me as a youth minister.

Or, maybe, this chapter will remind you that failing is not possible when you trust the G.O.A.T.

You see, as COVID-19 began to disrupt the church and the world, I did NOT pivot my ministry to "online" or "virtual" or "distance learning."

No Zoom meetings. In fact, no programming. I took a pause. A hard pause.

Don't get me wrong. I begged the Lord to reveal a path to me. Any path. Because "without youth ministry programs, how will teens encounter Jesus?", amiright? But, the truth was, I had no peace in pivoting to…doing something for the sake of doing something. There had to be another option.

Lying in my bed one morning I asked the Lord to hear me out:

Will I die?
Will my loved ones die?
Will I have a job?
Have I failed?

My emotions, my inaction, my conflict…I felt as though I were
losing. I was overwhelmed. Overwhelmed that I couldn't just
dodgeball my way around COVID-19. Overwhelmed by my fear.
Overwhelmed by my resistance to the Holy Spirit.

Holy Spirit: Do you trust me?
Me: Um…yes?

I was unprepared to handle the moment. However, as restrictions
were extended from weeks to months, my thoughts moved from
overwhelmed to focusing on survival. At first, it was survival until
"normal" returns. But a radical and ridiculous thought began
to come over me: What if pausing was about unlocking a new
opportunity, a new revival? What if that new opportunity needed
me to survive so it could grow and be watered?

Holy Spirit: Survive.
Me: How am I supposed to do that?

Rest. Resting was one part self-care. It was about making my
primary vocation primary. I enjoyed getting a good night's sleep,
having family dinner every night, working out every day, investing
in relationships, creating content. But the power in this season
of rest was in the retreat. Retreat as spiritual exercise. Retreat as
withdrawing from the hectic pace of the world all around me.

Jesus modeled this. He retreated (Luke 4:42), slept through a storm
(Mark 4:38), escaped from chaos (John 10:39).

God always wants to be close to me. The pandemic gave me
permission to let him. Resting created the space not only in my

calendar but in my heart to detach and enter in to the challenge of uncluttered, undivided worship.

Survival brings rest and through rest, growth and revival have a chance.

Me: What will surviving cost me?
Holy Spirit: What might you gain by surviving?

Learning. No conference, webinar, podcast, cohort, or book provided me with a game plan for doing youth ministry during a pandemic. I needed to take time to see the forest, and not only the trees. And, at the same time, I needed to learn more about the trees. Without programs to manage, I felt free to explore, starting with my own heart.

The pause revealed that my passion was on low battery and that I needed to recharge. Not just in the resting, but in the gaining of multidisciplinary insight and knowledge from theology, psychology, and sociology (to name a few).

Also, I wanted to learn how the upheaval of our daily lives affected three areas: family life, school, and spiritual practice. Social media was helpful in detecting trends. But it was the anecdotal experiences of people in the community that greatly tested my previously-held notions of effective ministry.

Putting the insight and the stories together gave me some clarity—and passion—for what was needed, not what was preferred. After resting, I also had practice in the power of surrender.

Letting go. Relational ministry has been the joy of my service to the church. There was a risk—and a sense of loss—in choosing to pause programming. How would teens handle this interruption? Would the pause be responsible for teens losing or growing their faith? Could the ministry recover or grow?

This is where trusting the Holy Spirit was the hardest, and my intentional and constant prayer most essential. Letting go was a confession that I am not the savior: Jesus is. Pope John Paul II was known to spend hours in prayer every day, even to the point of dismantling his very busy schedule. I wanted to emulate this.

Letting go really was really more of a partnership than a getting out of the way. I'm grateful that Our Lord thinks so highly of me to invite and prepare me to cooperate with him, especially in saying to me, "I got this":

> I planted, Apollos watered, but God caused the growth. Therefore, neither the one who plants nor the one who waters is anything, but only God, who causes the growth. The one who plants and the one who waters are equal, and each will receive wages in proportion to his labor. For we are God's co-workers; you are God's field, God's building.
> (1 Corinthians 3:6-9, NABRE)

Pat Villa has served as a youth minister, worship leader, content creator, Confirmation Prep director, and strategic planner for Catholic parishes and schools in San Diego, California, for over twenty years.

SECTION FIVE
WHAT WE'RE TRYING

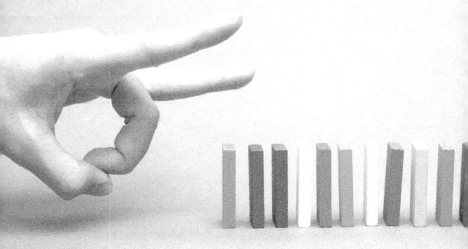

CULTURALLY CREATIVE, ACTIVELY AVAILABLE

By Mike Davis and Chaffawn Smith

We can all agree that the change 2020 has brought thus far has put most of us off balance. This sudden change has caused us to rethink what we have been doing for the past umpteen years. For some, this thought process has led to a time of revisioning our ministries, and for others, reorganizing some areas within our current ministries and program structures. But in our ministry to urban teens, we chose to ask God, "Lord, how would you have us respond in this season?"

When we started ministry in South Seattle three years ago, it was in response to the cry heard from the voices of youth in our community, articulating a need for a space where they would be heard and cultivated. With this cry ringing in our hearts, we rebuilt and rebranded our City Life program (Youth for Christ's ministry for urban teens) and called it Cultured.

Since its inception, Cultured's mission has been to cultivate creative spaces for youth to encounter community, opportunity, and the presence of God. We engage teens in performing arts, fashion, sports, job training, academic support, and just simply hanging out.

Before the world changed, we would have students hanging at our site three to four days a week, in the basketball gym, recording studio, dance studio, or just in our main area on gaming systems. Most students would return on Thursday evenings to participate in a weekly event called Cultured Nights. We learned quickly that the most important need for our young people was to be wanted, and to have people actively available and involved in their lives. Our programs served as opportunities and excuses to do just that: be actively available in ways that creatively met cultural needs.

I tell you all this to paint a picture of how we felt led to do ministry in the BC (Before COVID-19) days. Not that what we were doing was wrong or not led by God, but the pandemic had a way of reminding us of the original call God gave us here at Cultured: to be God's representation of his response to the issues our youth and their families were facing at an alarming rate. COVID-19 helped to magnify those issues.

If you were a student who was socioeconomically low-income, then you probably depended on school lunches for a meal every day, which was no longer available. You probably lived in a single-income home, and paying bills became even more of an issue than it was before. You were probably stuck at home with a parent who was frustrated and stressed out due to financial strains and other difficult circumstances. This could have also led to abuse as a result of the tension put on families in uncomfortable living spaces, trying to figure out this new norm. Of course, loneliness is an issue most of our students dealt with on a daily basis well before this pandemic. Now this is exacerbated as they have limited interactions with other teens and can only see friends on a screen through social media, trading authentic connections for artificial interaction. Oh yeah, let's not forget the social justice movements that took the world by storm, adding yet another layer of needed change in our communities.

Here's how we responded, in a creative way that culturally met needs in our community:

- **Virtual meetings** (yes, probably just like you). We met online in place of our Thursday night club, and these meetings were just as engaging online as they were in person. Through worship, games, and simply providing space for youth to vent and express themselves, we were given the opportunity to bring youth group into the homes of our young people, repurposing spaces that were full of stress and depression, turning them into youth sanctuaries for an hour and a half. We would see and hear families in the background as club was happening virtually. And, our youth ministry went from just a local ministry to a national ministry, as youth from other cities and states began to tap in with us.

- **Social media challenges with prizes and giveaways delivered to their front doors.** Also celebrating birthdays and checking in with students.

- **Small group hangouts, with food deliveries.** Just a way to keep youth actively involved.

- **Prayer walks throughout the community.** Since we no longer needed to have our space physically open every day, we had the freedom to be out in the community to walk the streets and just pray.

- **Serving lunches in the community.** Families were able to bring their kids to a set location and get groceries, books, clothes, and games for home activities.

- **Weekly family check-ins**, asking if there were areas of need where we could be of support.

- **Help with bills, food, and rent.** With the help of our donors we were able to start a COVID-19 Relief Fund to support our families in need.

- **Incident responders.** A team was formed in partnership with other local community organizations to provide assistance if and when incidents happened throughout the community.

- **Senior graduation.** We toured to all of our seniors' homes and celebrated them in their front yards with gifts and encouragement as they prepared for the next phase of their journeys.

- **Words of encouragement.** We were always coming up with creative ways to bring encouragement to youth and their families, whether it was online or through a text or phone call. Sometimes it was pulling up by the yard and just holding conversations through the car window. There was always a way to be encouraging and present.

What we found to be most important during these times of change—even if it meant we had to rethink, reorganize, or revision our ministries and programs—was to remember that the call remains the same. Our role is to continue to be the representation and response of the kingdom of God to the world around us. When it's all said and done, no matter what change looks like, we serve a God who is the same today, yesterday, and forever (Hebrews 13:8).

Mike Davis is the South Seattle Ministry Director for Cultured, a City Life chapter of Youth for Christ.

Chaffawn Smith was born and raised in Kansas City, Missouri. She did ministry for twenty years before moving to Seattle in 2018 to become a Program Director for Youth for Christ. She currently works creatively with urban students by sharing the gospel through dance, spoken word, music, and career development.

LATE-NIGHT TALK SHOW WITH COMMUNITY IMPACT

By Jim Gass

In August, when we would normally return to regular programming after breaking for the summer, our building was still closed and all group gatherings were prohibited. When we met as a youth group before the pandemic, we would check in with one another, play a game, and have a message or activity that pointed us toward Christ. In our new reality, I wanted to offer our group a way to experience these same things, while working within appropriate safety guidelines.

The most obvious solution was to use Zoom, which we tried for a little while in the spring. The problem we encountered was that so many of our kids had transitioned to using Zoom for school that it was the last thing they wanted to do for youth group, and our engagement reflected that. I didn't want to keep beating that dead horse, so I looked for something that would be different and engaging.

Late Night on Broadway (our church's name is Broadway UMC, so our program name was just a play on words) developed as a way to check in with our youth, play a silly game, and share a devotion or mission moment even while we can't get together as a full youth group. It is a prerecorded show that takes on the format of a late-night talk show along the lines of *The Tonight Show* on NBC or *The*

Late Show on CBS. We converted our youth room into the set for the show, complete with a host desk with microphone, guest chairs, and a nighttime cityscape background we found on Amazon. It's a little bit cheesy, and has a bit of a camp skit feel to it, but that is part of the charm and helps make it fun and accessible.

For each episode, we have one or two members of the youth group come on the show as guests to be interviewed. Much like when Jimmy Fallon is interviewing a celebrity about their new movie, we'll interview the youth and let them talk about how things are going with whatever sport or activity interests them. I have been amazed at the enthusiastic participation of our quieter kids, those who might rarely speak during full youth group gatherings. One member of our group started playing guitar about a year ago and volunteered to be a "musical guest" to share a song he had learned. This interview and feature segment is a way the kids can see what the other members of the youth group are doing, beyond social media. It also allows each member of the youth group, one at a time, to come and be in their church, which has been closed to them for the last six months.

Not only do youth get to showcase what they've been doing, I get to sit down with each person who comes on the show and do interview prep. This helps the youth think about what they'll want to say during the interview portion and makes them more comfortable. It has also turned into a great point of connection as I get to sit and just talk with the student (socially distanced, of course) about what's going on with them, what their worries are, what their needs are, and so forth.

At the end of each episode, we film a silly game. We did "Socially-Distant Jenga," where the Jenga blocks were set up on a table, and I played against our youth guest. The trick to making it socially distant was that we each had a long stick we had to use to push the blocks out. It was silly, and it mostly worked—and it was funny, which was really the goal. Game time could be any "up front" game that has two players. It provides a good note to end the show, and reminds them that church should be fun.

A vital part of *Late Night on Broadway* is the devotion segment. I offer a brief devotion or spiritual focus for the episode, usually when a late-night host would give their monologue. This part isn't long or deep but gives the youth a jumping-off point from which they can dig in more spiritually. One of the great things that happened during the devotion segment is that we were able to connect with a local mission organization.

When the first episode of *Late Night on Broadway* aired, one of the people who saw it was the Executive Director for a ministry called Family Promise. Family Promise provides housing to families experiencing homelessness. The director contacted me and offered to come on the show during our devotion segment to discuss ways that our youth group can help the organization. During her interview, she explained what homelessness looks like in our area, and gave us a few options for helping out. The one that really jumped out to me was what she called a birthday box.

She explained that when kids who experience homelessness have birthdays, Family Promise likes to give the family a small box with birthday supplies: cake mix, icing, a happy birthday banner, balloons, a note of encouragement, and a small game or toy. This is something easy for members of our youth group to put together at home and then bring by the church, and it can make a big difference in the life of another kid. Best of all, it's something we can do even while we can't do a "together" mission. Our partnership with Family Promise is one that we will be able to continue and develop after restrictions on in-person gatherings are lifted.

Late Night on Broadway is helping us find new ways to connect with members of our youth group, and it initiated what could be a lasting partnership with a local ministry. It has been so successful that we plan to continue producing episodes as part of our ongoing ministry strategy, even after we start meeting in person.

Jim Gass is the Director of Next Generation Ministries at Broadway United Methodist Church in Maryville, Tennessee. Jim oversees the

Youth and Children's ministries, and coordinates the filming and livestreaming of worship each week.

VIRTUAL SCHOOL STUDY HALL

By Megan Faulkner

I was sitting on a bench facing the ocean, about to baptize her fifteen-year-old daughter, when I pitched a mom an outside-the-box idea for this coming year. We had been waiting for two other girls and their families to arrive and had begun talking about what our ministry to middle and high school students could look like in the fall. I replied honestly to her question about this, saying, "I have no idea, except I have this thing I can't stop thinking about…"

"What is it?" she replied. That's when I told her all that had been swirling around in my head for weeks.

"Do you think this will work?" I asked trepidatiously once I'd finished.

"Do I think it will work?!" she replied with excitement. "I think it's brilliant!"

At the point of our conversation, nothing was on paper, nor on a whiteboard, chalkboard, smartboard, or in a notebook. The plan wasn't solidified or buttoned up, and there were certainly no bows tied on top. In all honesty, by the time you're reading this chapter we might have discovered that this plan has already failed miserably. The other families our ministry serves could think it's ridiculous, or the school schedule could have changed (again!), which would make this idea irrelevant.

Let me back up a bit before I get into our plan. Because this season comes with too many unknowns, some time ago I began a list of the things I do know:

1. Our ministry will continue to be a place that connects students to Jesus and each other.
2. We will continue to raise and empower generations of leaders to be world-changers.
3. We will provide space for all of that to happen, regularly, even amidst the disruption.

Student ministry always comes with its own challenges. However, student ministry in New Jersey—once in America's epicenter of a pandemic—has added to that list exponentially. Our ministry serves five middle schools and seven high schools, with only four of those schools being in the same district. This disjointedness adds significantly to the scheduling chaos in any year, let alone this one. While most of our schools are beginning 100% virtually, some have elected to do a hybrid in-person/virtual option, leaving students in school anywhere from two half days to four half days each week. Only two of our twelve total schools are providing five-day-a-week, in-person education. What a time to be the Chaos Coordinator—I mean, the Youth Pastor!

In praying about a solution, **I felt compelled to support families rather than continue to be a place that adds something to the schedule.** In doing so, I think what we're creating will end up serving the spiritual needs of teenagers as well as the physical needs of parents in terms of time alone to work from home.

Because of the fragile scheduling situation in our area, we're prayerfully hoping to offer dynamic programming that would allow students to encounter the love of Jesus and be cared for in practical ways. Historically, we've chosen to serve students a few days a week, allowing for the bulk of our ministry to happen on Wednesdays and Sundays. Because Sunday nights are not the only free night anymore, and sports and other extracurricular activities are not maintaining their once-robust schedules, this allows for some creative scheduling on our end. And we'll need creativity, considering the limitations on distance, number of people, and anything else that comes into play each day!

With all of that in mind, here's what I pitched to a few parents, our pastoral team, and our students and leadership:

What if we became the gathering place? The place that was open (safely)? The place where kids could come when they weren't in school, while their parents were working, and their afternoons were free? The place that they could count on to have an open door?

What if our open door led to virtual school classrooms where students could come plug in during the afternoon? What if the loneliness of virtual school was solved by us becoming a place where virtual school could happen, all together?

Our goal is to be open two or three afternoons a week for students to engage in virtual learning and homework, communally. We'll follow all of the guidelines by wearing masks inside, screening for health concerns, and practicing enhanced cleanliness standards. Students will be able to participate in their own schooling while being surrounded by their friends and youth leaders, and parents' afternoons will then allow for distraction-free work from home. **Think study hall—but fun—and with all of your friends.** Also, it will be really easy to invite other teenagers who aren't plugged in to our ministry yet—"Come do your virtual school work with us in this super cool space!" It may be convincing, right?

At the tail end of these open hours, we'll host small groups in the late afternoon through early evening, allowing families to be home for dinner. In surveying our families, most shared that they enjoyed the evening time all together at home that quarantine gifted. I've been compelled to support families, and scheduling our ministry time outside of anticipated family time seems to be the solution for that in this season.

Because students won't be attending school at all on Wednesdays in our area, Tuesday nights have become an opportunity for big-group fun. Together with our kids' ministry, we're hoping to have Tuesday family nights: town-wide capture the flag (we live in a beach town!), manhunt, running bases, and other outside activities that engage the whole family and the whole person, socially, emotionally, and spiritually.

I'm not sure any of this will actually work out the way I'm planning it in my head and (now) on our whiteboard, but I am convinced that creating space for peer togetherness and family togetherness is the absolute right thing in this season. Instead of competing with the school schedule, our team is committed to meeting families where they need us. Instead of saying, "come to us to do our thing," our heart for this plan communicates, "we're here for YOU, to help you do yours."

Megan Faulkner serves as the Director of Anchored Student Ministries for the Ocean Grove Church in Ocean Grove, NJ, where she is beginning her thirteenth year. More about Megan's ministry can be found at www.meganefaulkner.com.

ASYNCHRONOUS SPIRITUAL FORMATION

By Shannon LeMaster-Smith

My master's degree program was a hybrid of in-person and online classes. Some of the online classes required that we all log on at the same time and video chat after hearing our professor give a lecture in real time. This is called synchronous learning—when all students learn at the same time. Another form of online learning is asynchronous—learning at your own pace, on your own time. You can log in any time to do your work, listen to a prerecorded lecture, post on discussion boards, etc. This asynchronous format enabled me to be in school while working a full-time ministry position.

Before the pandemic, people's hectic schedules made it seem impossible to find one good time for every person to be in the same place at the same time—for worship, service, Bible study, fellowship, or even fun. Understanding this, my church's vision was to help people "develop habits of worship, prayer, and learning" (systems that people could use at home, on vacation, in the car, etc.). As part of this I've been developing a repertoire of spiritual formation practices that people can use anywhere, anytime. Utilizing multiple intelligences (the many ways that people learn and engage with content), I put together calendars and prayer stations for children, youth, and families to do together to grow closer together with God and with one another.

Calendars. People joke that the most useless purchase of 2020 is a planner. I once lived by mine, but it collected dust for a few months—until I remembered I could use the calendar to connect with people. I turned a monthly calendar into a spiritual formation resource that paralleled the sermon series for each month. Through conversations with the worship staff I came up with devotional prompts and activities to enhance the messages each week.

Sundays included our times for Zoom Sunday School and worship, along with the Scripture passages. My personal favorite, **Talk Tuesdays**, included an open-ended question for families to talk about together (I also posted this question each week in our church Facebook group). **Thankful Thursdays** invited people to reach out to a particular group of people to share encouragement and support. I adapted the themes for Mondays, Wednesdays, Fridays, and Saturdays to best fit the sermon series.

In May, our sermon series was "Upside Down," based on the Sermon on the Mount.

Make-It Mondays involved using your hands to make something (such as, "make something with salt" to go along with Matthew 5:13-20). **Wacky Wednesdays** encouraged doing fun things "upside down" or backward or in a different way. Fridays and Saturdays contained a mixture of service options, Scripture passages, journal prompts, and spiritual disciplines—all based on the message for that week.

For the month of June, the series was on movies. **Monday Movies** introduced the movie to watch for the next Sunday. **Word Wednesdays** contained a set of three words to look up the definition of and have a conversation about. **Fun Fridays** encouraged people to find some joy, as the pandemic restrictions didn't seem to be going away anytime soon. **Serve Saturdays** contained options for doing good in the community, such as "collect plastic grocery bags for the soup kitchen throughout the month of June," or "send someone an encouraging note in the mail."

The intent behind the calendars was NOT to provide yet another thing to *do*; rather, it was to encourage people to continue to grow as disciples even when we could not gather in person. The activities, Scriptures, and prompts could be done at anytime, anywhere, and with whomever. Knowing that others in the church were also doing them kept us connected as a congregation.

Prayer Stations. Prayer stations are a fabulous way to engage youth on multiple levels. They can incorporate art, visuals, body movements, tactile objects, nature, music, Scripture, and other mediums to connect us with God and with one another. Prayer stations invite us to slow down and make time for internal processing and reflection. Before the pandemic, I set aside time for us to do prayer stations, each at our own pace, followed by group reflection. Because of the pandemic restrictions, I set up prayer stations in our church garden, where people could come and go as they wished. I left the stations out for six weeks, checking regularly on supplies. I set up the activities so that people would still be able to see what those before them had contributed, in order to include a sense of connectedness to others. Signs in the front church yard invited anyone who walked by to participate. Here are two of those prompts:

Prayer
- 1 Thessalonians 5:17 (ESV) says, "Pray without ceasing." Prayer is like breathing; it is an ongoing connection to the Source of Life. We offer prayers to God as we offer our lives in service to God.

- Write a prayer on the fabric strip. Tie the prayer to the tree.

- As you look at the other prayers on the tree, know that we are all connected through prayer.

Grief
- We have all experienced loss during this pandemic. For some, it is the loss of a loved one. For some, it is the continuous cancellations of plans, events, and vacations. For others, it is the loss of physical touch and quality time with friends and family. Grief is the sense of loss or great disappointment, a burden.

- In Matthew 11:28 (NIV), Jesus says, "Come to me, all you who are weary and burdened..."
- Pick up a rough rock. Feel its rigid edges and think about what grief or disappointment you want to give to God. Place your rock in the water.

In this season of disruption, we can help youth develop spiritual disciplines and incorporate them into their everyday lives. They learn to experience God no matter where they are or who they are with, and at any time. This is truly a gift that will last beyond the time we have with them.

Shannon LeMaster-Smith is an ordained Deacon in the UMC and has served in youth ministry for over fourteen years. She is married to her best friend, Jonathan; together they have three dogs and live in Western North Carolina.

VIRTUAL CAMP FOR SMALL CHURCHES
By Vera Smith

Camp weeks and retreat weekends are a highlight of our church's youth ministry calendar. There's something so special about the buzz of getting a large group organized and dedicating hours to doing life together. This summer, we were not able to pile students into a van, travel across state lines, and spend the entirety of our ten-hour drive listening to *The Greatest Showman* soundtrack. However, we still had an amazing experience: virtual camp.

For over eighty years, small youth groups from five different states have partnered together to put on a summer camp. We could not imagine summer without this event—so we adapted it for life in a pandemic. While this specific model worked for our camp, perhaps some aspects of what went well will be useful for youth workers who are trying to figure out retreats in this season of disruption. Here is what each day looked like:

Morning Watch. At the start of the day, a prerecorded video was posted to our camp Instagram page. It consisted of a short message based on the theme, two worship songs, announcements, and a thought-provoking question for the day.

Tryst. After lunch, we asked the youth to take part in some quiet time called Tryst. The origin of the word comes from Middle

English and refers to an agreement to a secret or private meeting with someone you love. It's important for each of us to build the habit of scheduled prayer time. To help students engage in their quiet time with God, we provided written devotions—one for each day. At the scheduled time, a prerecorded video was posted on Instagram that included an introduction from an adult, a reflection from one of the youth, and a worship song. Then, there was an invitation to pause the video and take the time each person needed in quiet (or it would play soft music for five minutes).

This 'n' That. For a "pop-up" event during the early afternoon, we invited students on a Zoom call. For forty-five minutes, we had fun with a little bit of this and a little bit of that! Activities included screen games, foil sculptures, origami, an on-the-spot not-so talent show, and a scavenger hunt. This was an important connection piece—to be able to see faces and have fun with one another.

Evening Watch. Each night there was worship on Instagram Live, hosted on the camp account. We also incorporated an emcee each night to engage with students (who would respond using the chat feature).

Prayer Group. Youth were assigned Zoom prayer groups to meet with after Evening Watch. Each group consisted of two adult leaders and five to eight teens. The groups were arranged by gender and age—mixed in with all of the participating churches. After introductions and checking in on highs and lows for the day, we would spend time on the questions posed at Morning Watch and any reflections from the evening lesson.

Fun Extras. In order to build camaraderie between the youth while they were not physically together, we were sure to incorporate some fun competition. Everyone was split into two teams for the week—red versus blue. Teams could earn points in a few different ways:

- Showing up to the This 'n' That activities
- Winning the various challenges at This 'n' That

- Posting a photo for spirit days (hashtag your team color, tag the camp Instagram page)
- Posting a photo completing the daily challenge (tasks that involved serving family, friends, and community)

The emcee at Evening Watch would give updates on the red versus blue competition, keeping up the hype.

Social distancing restrictions are constantly changing. But one of the well-received ideas was "camp in a bag"! Leaders from each of the participating groups delivered gift bags to their students that included some camp essentials: their Tryst devotions in a folder with the camp schedule, a camp T-shirt, pens, glow sticks, candy, and a face mask. The groups that were able to gather picked a day or a few activities to meet outside for as they Zoomed with the other churches.

A professional praise band, well-known speakers, stage lights, and high-quality technology are all super impressive at a camp week or retreat weekend. But as youth workers, we know that the core of what really works in youth ministry is the relationships. At both our in-person conferences and this virtual camp week, we have done our best to capitalize on our unique position as small churches that have the ability to engage those relationships.

Teenagers need ample opportunity to verbalize their faith. One of the intentions behind our evening prayer groups was to give youth the space to process and ask questions—rather than just telling them what to believe and expecting them to somehow translate that to life at home. We tried to find multiple places where teens could articulate their faith and lead. We asked students to speak at Tryst and elected team captains to encourage participation in the red versus blue competition. Following the camp, we encouraged churches to provide a time for their teens to share with their home congregations what they learned and how they are growing.

What can you do with all of this? This season of disruption may make it feel like we need to scrap everything we know and start over. But I encourage you to hold on to the things that you know work well for youth ministry. One of the draws of a retreat is the opportunity for teens to see many peers from all different places on a similar faith journey. Don't cancel the retreat. It will look different. You may not be loading up the van, and you are probably utilizing social media and Zoom in ways you never imagined. But we can still embrace the designated time to unplug from our usual distractions and connect teens to a group of their peers and caring adults, and respond to the Holy Spirit actively at work.

Vera Smith is the Director of Children & Youth Ministry at Forest Hill UMC in Concord, NC. She is also a swim coach and lives in Kannapolis with her husband, Travis, and their dog, Henry.

INSTA DEVOS LED BY STUDENTS

By Matthew McNutt

When the world locked down, we scrambled to learn how to use Zoom, YouTube Live, and Instagram Live. Our small groups stayed strong despite being over Zoom, but honestly, this probably had more to do with relationships and hanging out than any focus on spiritual content. When we tried to have teaching content, we quickly saw our engagement vanish. It became apparent that trying to simply transfer what we normally do in person to online was not effective. Our isolated teens were starving for connection, not monologues from their youth pastor.

Like many of the best ideas in my student ministry career, the idea for Insta Devos came from my wife, Heather. Her observation? Our teens are naturals when it comes to interacting on social media; why not invite them to create short video devotionals that could be shared over our student ministry Instagram feed? Unlike their adult leaders, perhaps they would be effective in ministering online.

Here is the first text I sent out to a handful of students inviting them to be part of making Insta Devos:

Hey, it's McNutt! We want to change up what we're doing next week with the student social media stuff. One of the things we'd like to do is start posting short devo thoughts from students on our group

Instagram. It can go a lot of directions: a devotional thought, a favorite verse and why, something God is teaching you, etc. It could be thirty seconds long or it could be five minutes long, and it doesn't need to be elaborate or perfect! All that to say, you are one of a handful of students who came to mind immediately—would you do one? You could text or email the video to me and then we would post it to the student account one morning. Let me know what you think!

They were all excited to take part, and within a week we had half a dozen amazing videos. I added an "Insta Devos" logo, their name, and school grade to the videos, and then began uploading them three days a week to our Instagram IGTV feed and our Facebook page. The response was incredible. For comparison, had I uploaded a video of myself giving a short devotional thought, I would have been happy with a couple dozen views and maybe a comment if someone was feeling really generous. The student devotional videos? 400, 500, 700 views. The comments blew up. Friends were sharing them to their Instagram Stories. Other teens reached out wanting to submit videos as well. It was incredible.

Not only that, the videos got surprising traction on Facebook as well—just not with the students. As one of my teenage sons puts it, "that's old-people Instagram." Parents, grandparents, and, perhaps more importantly, many of our congregation members were blown away by the insights shared in the videos. An added bonus was that many of the students referenced what they were learning in their regular quiet times, unintentionally highlighting their spiritual habits. People I would have never expected to even be aware of our student page were sharing the videos and being moved by the faith of our teens. What we had hoped would be a way to keep kids spiritually plugged in was also becoming a way to open the eyes of our congregation to see the faith and leadership of our students.

It did not stop there. Other youth pastors, seeing me share the videos, reached out to ask how they could replicate the format in their groups. It's such a simple concept, yet it has great impact, especially in a time of isolation and disruption.

After our initial surge of student videos, we began to find that many of our students hadn't participated yet because they were intimidated. They didn't think they would be able to come up with something, or they were worried they would look bad. Wanting to set them up to win, I created a devotional guide based on the book of Ephesians. Basically, I split the book up into twenty-four short passages, wrote a short introduction for each passage, and then created three questions for each passage. I told students they could use as much or as little of my guide as they wanted. Those who were previously intimidated loved this simple resource. It gave them the confidence to know what to share. Their videos still were focused on their own insights—my questions simply gave them a direction in which to head. Others who were more confident ignored my guide and created their own responses to the passage. Either way, it was another success in our Insta Devos experiment: More students were able to participate, and more videos were shared.

Like many, last spring we were throwing things at the wall, hoping for something to stick. For us, this was a huge win, both in finding a way to get spiritual content out to our group, and in seeing the students who created videos take the opportunity to step up and allow their own leadership and faith to mature through it.

Matthew McNutt has been a youth pastor for twenty years. He is also a frequent author, speaker, and Pac-Man warrior. He and his wife, Heather, have four teenage sons and currently serve at Brandywine Valley Baptist Church in Wilmington, Delaware.

MEETING THE NEEDS OF OUR COMMUNITY
By Ebonie Davis

A few months into the pandemic, the COVID-19 impact sunk in for youth and adults alike. We are a small church with a large senior population, so we took an even more cautious approach to reopening than the local government required. The virus hammered our youth group. Several members drifted away, no longer entranced by the quickly-fading novelty of Zoom youth meetings. A small core group of mostly more mature youth hung on, along with a couple of displaced college students.

We've been through tough ministry seasons before, albeit with different triggers. I prayed the same soul-baring prayer I often whisper in desperate places: "Lord, I'm clueless. Please show me what to do now." The answer moved us back to basics. For weeks we focused on Matthew 22:37 and 39 (NIV): "Love the Lord your God with all your heart, and with all your soul, and with all your mind… Love your neighbor as yourself." What does it look like to love God during this pandemic? How do we love ourselves? How can we best love our neighbors right now? Having wrestled with the first two questions, the youth were primed to act on the third. The growing racial unrest coinciding with the pandemic intensified their focus. Which neighbors needed loving from us?

Immediately we shifted our priorities. It's like we tired of fixating on our pandemic coping strategies, burst out of ourselves, and focused our attention on how our neighbors were doing. The empathy among the youth overflowed as they considered others' experiences. This virus with all its necessary restrictions had left us feeling powerless and obsessed with loss. When compassionate love got a foothold, we stopped focusing on what was missing and concentrated on the resources we have.

What do we have? Well, a decent-sized parking lot, a handful of passionate teens and young adults, and a group of dedicated seniors—grandma-types, to be exact. How could we use these things, beyond Sunday mornings, to reach our pandemic-weary community? What would happen if we simply offered God our five loaves and two fish?[16]

When our county announced that the school year would start virtually, one pressing need of our neighbors became abundantly clear! This season has been challenging for most parents jolted into the homeschooling role, but especially so for working-class and immigrant families.

At the youth's urging, we quickly reimagined our cancelled fall events as "Love Your Neighbor Days." (One thing I love about students is that when they are passionate about something, they are unencumbered by details and logistics!) We focused on the neighborhoods directly on either side of us: one a largely Latino working-class mobile home park, the other a primarily African-American townhome community. Over the years we'd lost our connection with these neighborhoods, so what better place to start loving our (in this case, literal) neighbors? We resolutely replaced ineffective outreach tactics with intentional efforts to love them in meaningful ways. With a Good Samaritan mindset, we asked God which of their urgent needs brought on by the pandemic our small church could impact.

We took our events to their turf. Aside from being a safer alternative with smaller numbers, it was a more comfortable fit for our Latino neighbors. Our teens lovingly prepared playlists and simple, safe activities suited to each community. Like any good party, there was plenty of food, and we gave away supplies to help parents in their teaching roles. Most of all, we enjoyed and engaged our neighbors. We knew we were on the right track when some of the families brought out blankets to make a picnic for the afternoon! These events were far less elaborate than our normal fall fare, but far more fruitful in terms of the connections we made with people.

The Love Your Neighbor Days bridged to more opportunities to love and serve our community. Reflecting on what we had to offer, we used these events to launch Recess Days—a weekly opportunity for parents to drop their kids off for socially safe, outdoor fun on our parking lot. With no virtual schooling on Wednesdays, the day seemed like a natural fit for our neighbor-loving mission. Now we give parents a break by first feeding their kids and then running off some of their energy! Each week, kids look forward to a different theme, fun activities, and a kid-friendly gospel message. Maybe this ministry to parents and kids wouldn't be such a big deal if we were a big church with lots of resources, but for us it was a huge leap of faith!

As we prepared to launch these ministries, we got last-minute intel about a CARES Act grant from our county Health Department. They were partnering with local churches and nonprofits to support efforts to reduce the COVID-19 spread and share education. Our Recess Days, with their focus on COVID-19 safety, were right on target. We were awarded almost $30,000 to continue this community work. The ripple effects are amazing! Our drifting youth are wandering back to be a part of the ministry. New teens from the communities we engaged are showing interest. Intergenerational cooperation is making a comeback. The grant provided for a few temporary employees to help us in our efforts, so our young adults who were laid off or unable to return to college are now employed with this ministry. Most importantly, God's love and his good news are being shared where hope was becoming scarce.

Perhaps there is a similar program in your community (I encourage you to find out), but even if there isn't, don't miss the true miracle here. It isn't the grant that changed our COVID-19 mindset; it's God, honoring our faithfulness to love our neighbor, even in the midst of a pandemic. Like the boy who shared his lunch on that Galilean mountainside, God is blessing what little we had to offer, and he's using our youth and young adults to lead the charge.

Ebonie Davis is a veteran youth worker in a Maryland suburb of Washington, DC. She's contributed to a number of youth ministry books and articles and is the co-author of Disrupting Teens with Joy: Helping Youth Discover Jesus-Focused, Gritty Faith.

BRIDGING THE CHURCH TO HOME
By JJ Gibbs

During this season I have struggled to connect with students through my tried-and-true methods. Like many others, I found myself scratching my head on how I could possibly continue building relationships if we weren't physically together. So many times, I would simply not have an event because I couldn't initially conceive how to be in community without being face-to-face. After many meetings with my ministry leaders, multiple discussions with fellow youth ministers, and more prayer time than I have probably had in the last two years, I finally found the answer I was looking for. Honestly, it was plain and simple. The answer, for us, was to begin bridging the church to each student's home.

What better time than now to shake up our traditional methods and bring youth group and small groups to students at home? Small groups or life groups have always been elements I have wanted to develop in our youth ministry program, but ones that I could not, or would not, take the time to implement. COVID-19 gave me the time and kick in the butt to finally make them happen. We started small at first, doing what many of you did: Zoom meetings on Sunday nights for a quick icebreaker game, followed by a large group overview of our weekly lesson. Then we would use the awesome Zoom feature called breakout rooms for our small groups. This made ministry easier for me—getting to see my students, even if not in the usual way—and it also enabled our small group leaders to continue building relationships with our students.

As this started to take off, we added a Thursday game night, also on Zoom, where we would strictly play games and connect through technology. We were able to use skribbl.io[17] and various Jackbox Games.[18] Students could actively participate, versus just sitting and listening to me talk. All of this combined to provide us with a good foundation to continue on what I then thought would be a short journey.

In ministry, it is not a good idea to get too comfortable with what you are currently doing. When we got to month two of the virus shutdown (the month of May, for us here in North Carolina), I started to notice a drop in attendance across the two nights we were meeting. I couldn't understand what we were doing that would cause students to not want to show up. I had one brave student who would call me every week before our meeting. Each time she would say that she loved me and missed me but would not be attending the evening's event. This floored me every time. Why would she take the time to call me, but not take the time to join our Zoom meetings? The obvious answer, one many of you realized around the same time I did, was that my students were *tired of being online*! In a culture where technology seems to be the driving force, I found myself in a new world where teenagers had finally had enough. Each day they would sit in front of their computers for class and then I would turn around and ask them to jump back online to learn some more.

I found myself reevaluating once again, always remembering what I was called to do: bridge the church to students' homes. We noticed that our students were craving human interaction and conversations. What we didn't know was how to navigate the everyday struggles in our teenagers' lives. I started creating different ways to show love and appreciation. One of them was creating yard signs that simply said, "We Love Our Students." Placing these signs in each student's yard gave us the opportunity to advertise for our youth ministry, but more importantly it gave me the chance to catch up with each student. Driveway visits became my favorite thing to do by far. They allowed me to see our teens in their home environments and learn more about them and their parents. These visits also gave us the idea of bridging our high school ministry with our college ministry to have Dinner Supper Club once every other month in someone's home (backyard, usually), beginning this fall.

We also began a curriculum change during all of this. Our ministry had been using good curriculum before, but it was not emphasizing the overall goal we had for family ministry growth. We decided to switch to Orange Curriculum, which has allowed us to not only help lead and build the faith of our teenagers but also minister to the faith of our leaders and parents. Switching to this curriculum helped emphasize the meaning of bridging the church to home because it allows for whole-family growth in their faith journeys at home, where I cannot always be.

With every day I find myself evolving and learning new things, continuing to focus our ministry on bridging the gap between the church and home. Ministry cannot always be done within the confines of our youth room with all its awesome luxuries. Sometimes it must happen through technology or at each one of our students' homes. Wherever we are, we know that God is with us on each step of the way.

JJ Gibbs is the Director of Youth Ministry at Jamestown United Methodist Church in Jamestown, NC. He lives in Asheboro, NC, with his wife, Christina, daughter, Maylin, and new puppy, Ridge. JJ has been involved in ministry for over a decade, with the last five years focused on youth.

REFOCUSING ON SERVING
By Rhiannon Kelly

As a coping mechanism for dealing with all the things cancelled this year, especially our mission trips, I started writing thank you notes to COVID-19, a concept borrowed from Jimmy Fallon: *"Thank you, COVID-19. Because of you, I will not have to sleep on an air mattress more often than my own bed this summer; I will not have to write up any accident reports; I will not get awakened at 2 a.m. because a youth's bunkmate is vomiting everywhere from eating too much pizza; I will not have to send the same parent twelve emails and twenty-seven texts just to get one permission form signed; I will not have to herd youth, who are similar to cats, through international airports this summer."*

In all seriousness, when we made the call to cancel our youth summer mission trips and kids' camp and VBS (where our youth are the lead volunteers), I mourned, realizing the gaping holes to come. Our summers are defined by youth being in service. Through summer service, their hearts and minds are changed, their relationship with God grows as they are disconnected from their normal realities, and youth create lasting bonds and memories. It is incredible to bring transformed youth home to their parents.

The summer mission trip and activity cancellations came at the point where my surge of pandemic adrenaline was wearing off;

youth were already Zoomed-out, families were heading off on vacations, and virtual attendance had plummeted. It was clearly time to refocus on service. I felt certain the Holy Spirit—coupled with an Incredible Hulk mentality of smashing every obstacle in my way—would guide me to provide opportunities for our youth to grow stronger in their walk with Jesus through safely serving, even during a global pandemic. It would be critical to find socially distanced and outdoor projects that would satisfy public health guidelines as well as parents' comfort levels.

I began to identify the current needs in our community, in our church congregation, and with our local partner agencies. I hoped we could offer new and creative opportunities, coupled with familiar ones, for our youth and leaders to connect with each other, our congregation, God, and others. My goal was to propel us forward together in the ministry.

We started by inviting youth to come to our church's front porch to assemble the daily bags each child would receive for at-home VBS. Next, we partnered youth with families to be their masked personal helpers for VBS. Youth sat on decks and in driveways with kids as they tuned in to our live, virtual streaming of VBS each evening. They were our personal hype team! Our youth got the kids excited, taught them the songs and dances, guided them in craft activities, helped them with the mission projects, and enjoyed snacks together. Our final evening of VBS was an in-person event where youth came to set up an assembly line for our mission project of packing bags of school supplies we had collected for kids in our community.

The following week—Monday through Friday—youth participated in nine different mission projects in our Youth Week of Local Service. This was our first time offering youth a full week of service in our community. We picked opportunities all over town where youth were able to safely serve in outdoor settings and where parents or youth could drive themselves, with options for both mornings and evenings to accommodate their varying schedules.

- We painted soccer goals for an agency that serves kids in

underprivileged neighborhoods and helped organize donated jerseys and cleats in their field house.

- We shopped for groceries for newly-arrived refugee families in need.
- We cut fresh flowers and made arrangements that were delivered to some of our older church members. (For weeks after, I received beautiful handwritten thank you cards for this!)
- We helped clean up and beautify a community park.
- We partnered with another local church to package meals to be delivered in surrounding neighborhoods.
- We assembled very personalized fun activity bags for our special needs kids in our "Buddy Break" program. (This was all organized and led by a high schooler who is very involved with the program.)
- We helped clean the playground for an organization that serves refugees and immigrants and gave them some of the school supply bags we assembled at VBS.
- We delivered donations of Amazon wish-list items for a Cat Cafe and hung out with the rescue cats there.
- We had a final gathering and debriefing over pizza at a local restaurant.

Refocusing on service this summer led me to analyze our youth ministry with a different perspective. Through this time of disruption and the forced refocus, we experienced:

Rebirth of our youth ministry values with serving being at the crux of our ministry, empowering youth to lead in their areas of interest and strength.

Reimagining of serving in the future with a focus on local service occurring more frequently throughout the year. (We have twelve different local service projects lined up for the first two months of fall!)

Reconnection with youth, youth leaders, community partners, our church congregation, and parents.

Reenergizing our youth and youth leaders (including me!) about our ministry and the idea of service as an act of living out our faith together.

During our newly established "back to school" visits to youth, I went to see a middle schooler named Ally. We reminisced about the teepee we built during the Youth Week of Service. We had arrived on the project site and were given a pile of sticks, giant bamboo shoots, rope, and no instructions, and asked to make a teepee for kids to safely play in. Ally and I lamented about how difficult it was and laughed at how we thought we'd finally done it right—and then it collapsed into pieces the moment I was taking a picture! We talked about how we didn't think we would actually finish the project in time and recalled how I had scrambled to find a YouTube video on "How to Build a Teepee." With that bit of guidance, a lot of teamwork, and a desire to see the end result be a meaningful and safe space for others, we eventually built it successfully. Looking back, I see this teepee as a perfect representation of our refocused summer of service. Before I left, Ally and I agreed we both will still be in prayer for that teepee to stay upright, strong and supportive.

Rhiannon Kelly has been working in youth ministry for over eight years and currently serves as the Director of Youth Ministry at West Market Church in Greensboro, NC. She is passionate about service, social justice, and walking alongside teenagers in their lives and faith.

RETHINKING CONFIRMATION
By Ryan Schaible

"But it's a tradition!"

Every ministry leader has had to respond to those words—for better or for worse. Sometimes, however, traditions, represent not just a favorite program, but also a spiritual landmark that has spanned generations.

When everything changes, how do we keep the sacred traditions meaningful?

In our denomination (I am part of a Lutheran church), we have the yearly ritual of confirmation. For my more non-denominational or evangelical friends, confirmation is an opportunity for students to publicly profess their own faith in Jesus Christ. It is an experience deeply rooted in church tradition and theology.

When our day-to-day lives shifted almost exclusively online, we as a staff found ourselves having to initially postpone most of our spring events, including the annual Confirmation Service. This became a unique opportunity to completely rethink what confirmation is and what it could be, while still honoring one of our deepest-rooted church traditions (and trying our best to fulfill the expectations of students and families).

Instead of one large service, we chose to host *six* smaller online events over several days. This change proved to be about more than just meeting online versus meeting in person. It unearthed several exciting opportunities. In rethinking confirmation, we saw three major shifts happening:

1. Shifting the focus from CORPORATE to DEEPLY PERSONAL. Confirmation is a chance for individual students to profess their own faith in Jesus Christ, and this is done in the presence of friends, family, and other church members. It's a significant, shared experience for the whole church. Rethinking confirmation meant that while we could still gather online, we wanted to create smaller events for students and their families. Our students sat on living room couches or around the dinner table with their parents, while friends and family from all over the country were able to log in and join them. Doing several smaller events allowed for a personal, intimate connection for each group of students. You could see everyone on the screen. Even if it was just for half an hour, we all felt a little more connected (and a little less alone) during the services.

2. Shifting leadership from CHURCH STAFF to PARENTS. Normally, our confirmation service requires lots of advanced planning, and many of these responsibilities are shared by church staff members and volunteers. I have to print handouts, run the sound and lights, lead the music, set up a reception for afterwards, and then lead all of the other elements of the service. The actual service typically fills an afternoon. Rethinking confirmation meant that we shifted the serving focus from church staff to parents. While different staff members still had roles to play, we gave the most sacred responsibilities to parents. We invited parents to each pray out loud for their child—and they did it! Parents offered heartfelt, personalized blessings. There was never a dry eye on the screen during these services. Rethinking confirmation allowed parents to be deeply involved in the experience, not just passive attendees. Living rooms became sanctuaries. Dinner tables became altars. Parents became empowered to continue to be (or perhaps finally become) the primary spiritual leaders in the lives of their sons and daughters.

3. Shifting from GOING TO CHURCH to BEING THE CHURCH. It can be easy to compartmentalize our lives. Church is for Sunday mornings, right? Maybe add in a midweek service if you're super spiritual. This compartmentalizing is something we as ministry leaders battle against all the time. I *love* the tradition of confirmation and what it represents, but it can fit a bit too nicely into the compartment mindset if we are not careful: Fulfill the expectations, go to the service, say the right words, and make Grandma happy along the way—then you can move on with the rest of your life. The COVID-19 pandemic took a sledgehammer to our patterns of compartmentalization. We no longer had *church* and *home*. Church was at home; home *was* church. This disruption gave us the opportunity to present confirmation not as a singular service, not as a graduation event, but rather as a milestone moment on an ongoing journey of faith. As we made the first two shifts, the third moved into the spotlight. You logged in at home, and when you signed off you were still at home. You didn't "go" to church as a family—you *were* the church as a family. We designed the liturgy of the service to highlight this important fact. Every word spoken pointed beyond the digital service to a larger truth about what it meant to be the church.

"But it's a tradition!"

If you are part of a denomination that practices confirmation, I hope this is useful for you. If your theology and practice is different from mine, your church still has some type of tradition—that thing (or perhaps several things) that you just *have* to do in your ministry. Traditions are not inherently evil. I love tradition. We are all part of a larger Christian tradition. Traditions can help show what we care about and where our values can be found. But if you have a tradition that isn't working, get rid of it. And if you have a tradition (like confirmation) that maintains its meaning for your church, don't be afraid to *rethink it*. You'll find opportunities to dig a deeper meaning out of the tradition, allowing the people you serve to experience God in new ways. Leverage the disruption. Shifting and rethinking will bring you a new depth of insight into what it means to truly *be* the church.

Ryan Schaible serves as the Director of Family Life for Student Ministries at Good Shepherd Church in Naperville, IL. Ryan is a fan of Wisconsin sports teams, has been involved in youth ministry for nearly two decades, and holds an MA in Christian Formation and Ministry from Wheaton College.

ADDRESSING DEEPER NEEDS
By Dustin Dick

During the second half of my ten years in youth ministry I came to realize the need for ministry beyond what most youth workers are trained in or prepared for. As I finished up my master's in social work degree, I also made the transition from paid youth worker to a volunteer youth worker. I continue to use my skills from youth ministry in my social work career and have found that what I learned on my journey to becoming a social worker is just as important, if not more, than what I learned in Bible college. The youth pastor I volunteer under is excited about my training, and has encouraged me to use my social work background in our youth ministry.

Addressing our students' deeper needs has never been more important. I hope through the chaos of this pandemic, we will gain insights that will radically change the face of youth ministry.

Good youth workers often have minimal office hours, as our primary "place of work" is out with students: going to sporting events, attending band or choir concerts, meeting students for a coffee. We connect in the real world, which provides opportunities to see students in their natural habitats, show them we care for them beyond the church walls, and build relationships. During the pandemic, it's been so challenging to live into this aspect of our work, with students' events being cancelled and parents understandably reluctant to even allow their teens to meet us for coffee. Which leaves us with a question: How do we continue to build relationships when it's difficult to meet face-to-face?

One answer is to have virtual office hours. While it's not ideal—considering that many students experienced Zoom burnout and don't want to be online—making consistent virtual office hours known offers a virtual "drop-in" option for those who need to chat, or just want to hang out.

I had one particular student who really took advantage of this during the summer. He would regularly log in to my virtual office and hang out. He was a man of few words, and would typically sit and play on his PlayStation while I talked to him. Other times, we sat there together, existing in one another's world. After being stuck at home, it was nice to have an opportunity to reach out and connect to someone, having the feeling of being in the same room with someone else, even if both of us were participating in different activities.

I was fortunate to be able to utilize a telehealth platform for these office hours, which helped to eliminate the potential of any unwanted guests. I continue to have students drop in the room sporadically. One student recently logged in and claimed it was an accident. I know there are students who want to have someone to talk to, someone willing to listen, and they are curious if I am really going to be there.

During this time, many teenagers are experiencing an increase in depression, anxiety, stress, and loneliness. Navigating middle and high school can be challenging enough. Having to do so during a pandemic—when the expectations change each week—can be overwhelming. Screen time is way up (not only because of Zoom meetings), and sleep patterns are often dramatically changed. Teens need structure and some sense of order if they're going to thrive. With structure and order often missing during this season, many teens could use help in order to gain a sense of control and lessen anxiety and stress.

This summer, I led a "Coping with COVID" group. I met with students online each week to discuss anxiety, loneliness, dealing with loss, procrastination, developing creativity, the new school year, and what to expect next. When you have these discussions, the purpose should not be to diagnose a student or have all the answers, but instead, to continue to do life with them. Let your students know that their feelings of anxiety are perfectly normal and that they are not expected to know how to manage these feelings.

When teenagers are anxious, they are often more willing to look to the adults in their lives for answers. We need to normalize their feelings. Let your students know that anxiety is normal, and it serves the purpose of alerting us to potential threats. If appropriate, assure them these feelings of anxiety, depression, and stress are not necessarily signs of deeper problems or mental disorders, but rather their body and mind attempting to grasp what is happening.

If you are in over your head and cannot adequately navigate these waters, reach out to your congregation and see what resources you may have. Find a specialist, a counselor or therapist, a teacher, or someone else who has experience and training in this field. While these individuals would make a great addition to your youth ministry leadership team, that's not necessarily your goal. Instead, consider having them join you for a special lesson or series to talk about mental health and how to manage it, utilize coping skills, and what to do if it becomes too much for them. Or, simply ask these people to be occasional resources for you, providing insight and helping you know how to evaluate when a student needs a referral to professional help.

A couple years ago, I started ending any youth gathering with a quote from Christopher Robin, spoken to his dear friend Winnie the Pooh. I have carried this practice into my social work world and use it to encourage the families I work with. It sure feels like a fitting encouragement for these times: "You are braver than you believe, stronger than you seem, smarter than you think, and loved more than you know."[19]

Dustin Dick lives with his wife, Crystal, and their fur babes, Houdini Nagini and Lexi LouAnn, in Independence, Missouri. Dustin has been involved in ministry since the late 2000s and currently works as an in-school therapist and behavioral interventionist. He is a kids/youth volunteer at his church.

26

INTERACTIVE WHOLE-FAMILY WORSHIP
By Jen Bradbury

"I don't want to go to worship!"

During my tenure in youth ministry, teens have told me this more times than I can count; more times, in fact, than I'd like to hear. Teens don't want to go to worship because they find the sermons long, boring, or irrelevant—or some combination of all three.

The pandemic has magnified these cries. About three months into the pandemic, the outcry from my teens against virtual worship reached a dull roar that grew even louder when their parents joined in. Exhausted and overwhelmed, parents were no longer willing to fight their teens to participate in virtual worship.

"Teens are tired of screens," their parents lamented, even as their teens sat in another room playing video games or watching movies.

Clearly, teens aren't tired of screens, they're just tired of virtual worship (and virtual school, of course). And let's face it, "participating in virtual worship" is a bit of an oxymoron anyway. We don't participate in virtual worship. We consume virtual worship in the same way we consume a movie or TV show.

No wonder my teens don't want to be a part of it.

I don't want to be a part of it.

Knowing this, my team and I decided to reexamine worship. Our goal was to design a virtual worship experience for families that would facilitate connection between people of all ages, from toddlers through grandparents and everyone in between, including teens. We knew this would be no small feat, but we certainly thought it was possible.

To meet our goal, we realized we couldn't rely on prerecorded or even livestream worship. Instead, we turned to Zoom, which has quickly become both the nemesis and hero of so much of our pandemic church life. We decided to begin offering monthly live Zoom worship services.

Before our first one, we laid aside all of our pent-up frustrations and reevaluated Zoom, searching for what we could leverage for connection. Polls, chats, reactions, and even breakout rooms all became devices for us to use in worship to connect people with one another.

With the reluctant support of our senior leadership, our team—me, our music director, our children's choir director, and a handful of lay people committed to seeing families worship together—threw out everything we thought we knew about worship and began planning from scratch. We took each element in our traditional worship service and asked, "How can we use this to help people connect?" "How can we use this to engage people of all ages?"

The result is unlike anything I've ever been a part of in my nearly twenty years of ministry.

Our monthly live Zoom worship services are truly interactive. We encourage everyone to turn on their cameras so that we can see one another during worship, just as we'd see one another if we were actually worshipping at church together.

We write responsive readings. Then, we actually unmute people and allow them to read their short responses. The result is a beautiful cacophony of voices. We use polls to survey people in real time. We invite people to use their thumbs up and applause to react to what's going on at any given moment in the service. We invite (and model) use of the chat.

My pastoral colleagues and I co-write dialogical sermons for live Zoom worship. These dialogues occur between us. But even more importantly, they're between us and the congregation. Throughout the sermon, we pose questions to our parishioners and invite them to chat in their responses. For those with nonreaders in their families, we remind them to consult with their kids first to make sure their response reflects the thoughts of even their youngest family members. This creates faith-filled conversations during worship. As preachers, we then react to and even incorporate what people say in the chat into our sermon in real time.

Sometimes, to make the sermons even more family-friendly, we ask people to stop by the church before live Zoom worship to pick up something tactile that we then use. Prior to one live Zoom worship, we distributed pinwheels. We then talked about how the Holy Spirit is like wind and asked people to write or draw various things on their pinwheels before planting them in their yards as a reminder of how the Holy Spirit moves in our lives.

Thanks to chat, our prayers of the people actually come from our people. (Yep, we totally stole this from The Youth Cartel's Church for Youth Workers.) We give people prompts related to the day's theme and ask them to type in a prayer. We then invite them to read everyone's prayers as their own act of prayer. We end by saying "Amen" as a congregation.

Finally, we also continue to invite people, especially our teens, into worship leadership. During live Zoom worship, teens lead by reading Scripture passages, introducing the passing of the peace, sharing their musical gifts (either live on Zoom or by introducing a prerecorded video), or by participating in skits written specifically for the virtual space.

Following worship, we divide everyone into ten-minute breakout rooms to enable people to further connect with one another. Teens have conversations with elderly adults they never would have had on a Sunday morning because they would have been too focused on their own friends. Now, thanks to Zoom worship, they've made new friends from different generations.

These redesigned worship services aren't perfect. Not by a long shot. But what we've learned is that in pandemic life, people are willing to sacrifice perfection for connection.

And no one—not even our teens—complains that live Zoom worship is boring, irrelevant, or long. People have even begun to say these services aren't just workable for now: They're better than what we used to do in person in our sanctuary because they allow for more genuine, faith-centered engagement between people of all ages.

More impressive still? One of the people making that claim is our senior pastor.

Jen Bradbury is the Minister of Youth & Family at Atonement Lutheran Church in Barrington, IL. She's the author of several youth ministry books including The Jesus Gap *and* The Real Jesus.

ENDNOTES

1. Craig S. Keener, *A Commentary on the Gospel of Matthew* (Grand Rapids, MI: Eerdmans, 1999), 427.

2. See Sean McDowell, *The Fate of the Apostles: Examining the Martyrdom Accounts of the Closest Followers of Jesus* (New York: Routledge, 2015), 47-48.

3. Tertullian, *Apology*, 3:47.

4. Some of the early church fathers from the second and third centuries are called Apologists, such as Irenaeus and Justin Martyr, because they defended the Christian faith against internal and external criticism.

5. Justo Gonzalez, *The Story of Christianity: The Early Church to the Dawn of the Reformation*, Vol. 1 (New York: HarperCollins, 2010), 141-143.

6. C.S. Lewis, "Learning in War-Time," *The Weight of Glory and Other Addresses* (HarperSanFrancisco, 1980), 62-63. This insight was brought to my attention through the blog at the *C.S. Lewis Institute*: Joel S. Woodruff, "A Perspective on the Pandemic from C.S. Lewis." https://www.cslewisinstitute.org/node/4865 (accessed September 6, 2020).

7. Reggie Joiner and Kristen Ivy, *It's Just a Phase—So Don't Miss It: Why Every Life Stage of a Kid Matters and at Least 13 Things Your Church Should Do About It* (Cumming, GA: Orange Books, 2015).

8. Claire Pomeroy, "Loneliness Is Harmful to Our Nation's Health." *Scientific American.* March 20, 2019. https://blogs.scientificamerican.com/observations/

loneliness-is-harmful-to-our-nations-health/ (accessed September 7, 2020).

9. David W. Blight and Lucas Johnson, "America's Call for a Modern-Day Civil Rights Movement." Interview by Meghna Chakrabarti. *WBUR: On Point.* June 9, 2020. https://www.wbur.org/onpoint/2020/06/09/america-modern-day-civil-rights-movement.

10. "Year at a Glance: Membership Diversity." *Church Trends.* https://church-trends.pcusa.org/overall/pcusa/diversity/.

11. See Andrew Root, *The End of Youth Ministry?: Why Parents Don't Really Care About Youth Groups and What Youth Workers Should Do About It* (Grand Rapids, MI: Baker Academic, 2020).

12. To clarify, I don't think Andy is saying joy in youth ministry is individualized. I'm simply expounding upon his work.

13. These are a couple of articles that go into more depth on catastrophic thinking issues: Margarita Tartakovsky, "Catastrophic Thinking: When Your Mind Clings to Worst-Case Scenarios," https://psychcentral.com/blog/catastrophic-thinking-when-your-mind-clings-to-worst-case-scenarios/ and Laurie Ferguson, "The Signs of Toxic 'Worst-Case Scenario' Thinking, and How to Shut it Down," https://creakyjoints.org/living-with-arthritis/worst-case-scenario-thinking/. For further help on Revelation, I recommend BibleProject: https://bibleproject.com/explore/revelation/.

14. This list is inspired by Carey Nieuwhof's article, "The 5 Kinds of Church Leaders We're Seeing Right Now (And Their Future Prospects)." *Carey Nieuwhof.* https://careynieuwhof.com/the-5-kinds-of-church-

leaders-were-seeing-right-now-and-their-future-prospects/.

15. Sisters of Life, "Litany of Trust." *Sisters of Life.* https://sistersoflife.org/wp-content/uploads/2019/05/Mobile-Litany-of-Trust-English-1.pdf.

16. Reference to John 6:1-14 (NIV).

17. https://skribbl.io/

18. www.jackboxgames.com

19. Karl Geurs (director), *Pooh's Grand Adventure: The Search for Christopher Robin.* (Motion picture on DVD.) Walt Disney Television Animation. 1997.